After She was Born A Girl

From me to you
We are called to:
"Learn to do right, seek justice &
depend the oppressed" (Isaiah 1:17)

With love

Emmanuel Kaghondi
Tampa, FL.
Oct. 2023

A recollection of true events

(All names of individuals and certain locations have been changed to protect privacy.)

After She Was Born A Girl

A Memoir of Gender Injustices
in a Male-Dominated Society

EMMANUEL KAGHONDI

RESOURCE *Publications* · Eugene, Oregon

AFTER SHE WAS BORN A GIRL
A Memoir of Gender Injustices in a Male-Dominated Society

Resource Publications
An Imprint of Wipf and Stock Publishers
199 W. 8th Ave., Suite 3
Eugene, OR 97401

www.wipfandstock.com

PAPERBACK ISBN: 978-1-6667-7587-7
HARDCOVER ISBN: 978-1-6667-7588-4
EBOOK ISBN: 978-1-6667-7589-1

VERSION NUMBER 083023

To my wife, whose unwavering commitment to empowering women has been a perpetual source of inspiration for me.

To my mother, whose timeless legends still resonate with me to this day.

And to all African women who were born with an innate strength and resilience.

"We cannot solve our problems by deceiving ourselves
that they do not exist."

—Mwalimu Julius K. Nyerere.

Contents

—

Preface | ix

Acknowledgements | xi

The Woman behind the Shadow | 1

"If you are not dead, you are not formed" | 6

"If you don't know how to die, visit the graveyard" | 20

"When two bulls fight, the grass is what suffers" | 36

"Speak the truth or swallow a rock?" | 49

"A man's poo is inodorous" | 58

"Let him marry another wife" | 68

"Because He Is a man" | 79

And She Is a Woman | 90

The Uphill Battle for Change | 101

Forbidden Dreams to Pursuing Womanhood | 107

A Bird with No Wings | 116

(Un)celebrating Memory | 133

Bibliography | 137

Preface

—

I INVITE YOU TO embark on a journey that will take you through a range of emotions, from heartbreak to perseverance, from tears to laughter, from anger to romance. As you bear witness to the harsh reality of the most agonizing circumstances that plague the lives of women in Tanzania, brace yourself to confront uncomfortable truths about womanhood in a deeply entrenched patriarchal society. This journey will challenge you to question your long-held beliefs about justice and equality, and to reimagine womanness in a modern world.

The path ahead is far from easy, but it is a necessary one. It highlights the intricate intersection of cultural practices, memory, trauma, and spirituality that shape the lives of those who are too often silenced. Yet, when I started to write this book, I never meant it to be a critique of African cultural practices. I wrote it as a jubilant celebration of the unbreakable spirit and unwavering resilience of African women.

As a male writer, it is a peculiar irony that I have even penned these pages. It is not my place to claim ownership of these experiences but to bear witness to them and to hold them with care. The manuscript has followed me for over two decades, from humble notebook to multiple computers and flash drives. The very nature of my role as a man in a woman's world, and as an insider examining it from an etic perspective, led me to contemplate erasing every digital trace of this work let alone publishing it. Yet, a culmination of years of self-argument, discomfort, and dilemma has proven that some memories seek to be remembered.

Writing this book was like attempting to create a masterpiece with words. The daunting task was to capture the complexity and nuance of the deeply troubling experiences of the courageous women whose stories

I must share. In every keystroke, I was constantly reminded of the limitations of language in fully conveying the depth of human experiences. Transforming experiences into words was like an artist contemplating how to represent the intricacies of life on canvas. In the same way, I grappled with the challenge of doing justice to the raw emotion and physical pain of women's suffering through mere words. It became clear that simplified symbols could never truly capture the profound realities of the unheard. Nonetheless, I endeavored to paint a picture that would honor these stories and inspire others to take action towards love, justice, and equality.

As you open the pages of this book, I invite you to embark on a journey that will require an open mind and an open heart. You will be called upon to confront your assumptions and biases and to bear witness to the stories of those whose voices have been marginalized for far too long. Through these stories, you will gain a deep appreciation for the meaning of life, humanity, and dignity and be inspired to take action towards creating a more just and equitable world within yourself. I believe that this book will spark important conversations that will start from within ourselves and ripple outwards, leading to meaningful change in the world around us. Let us together embark on this journey of self-reflection, growth, and action.

Acknowledgements

—

WITH UTMOST HUMILITY AND gratitude, I offer my heartfelt acknowledgement to those who have journeyed with me on this literary path.

Foremost, I owe an immeasurable debt of gratitude to my beloved wife, Deborah Lyanga. Her unwavering support, boundless love, and steadfast commitment to women's empowerment and girls' rights have been an ever-present source of inspiration in both my life and this work.

My sincerest appreciation goes to those who have read the early versions and glimpses of this manuscript, providing invaluable comments and feedback that have shaped the evolution of this work. Your insights have been like rare jewels that have helped to refine and polish this story. In particular, I extend my deepest gratitude to Joan Vorkoper and Angie Genring, whose passionate interest in the initial craft these pages provided the necessary push to publishing this work.

To the women whose stories I have been privileged to share, I remain humbled by your courage, strength, and resilience in the face of unspeakable adversity. Your experiences have stirred my soul and compelled me to view the world through a new lens. It is my sincere hope that this book will serve as a tribute to your experiences, amplify your voices, and inspire others to join the fight for justice and equality.

I

-

The Woman behind the Shadow

—

NYASEMA, MY MOTHER, IS a mighty *mugumo* tree, defiantly standing tall amidst the barren landscape of existence. Her enigmatic grace and breathtaking beauty evoke a sense of awe and reverence. Meeting her is encountering a goddess in her very being. Her poise and elegance, the radiance of her charming smile and biting wit; the weaving of wisdom from time-tested legends and proverbs fills the cultural voids. Yet, beneath her glittering façade lies a secret, hidden within the tinted memories of her glory days. Her pulchritude is beyond a symbol of irresistible elegance behind a veneer of normalcy. This last mythic countenance has always fooled many of the overlooked woman in the inside. Even when the rooster crows, announcing an impossible morning, from her tattooed thin cheeks to her string of beads, Nyasema has succeeded to maintain a youthful hope that defies despair, a testament to the inner strength that lies within her kind.

Children, especially girls, found her charm irresistible. Every morning, they scrambled over the dewy grass, hastening to occupy their places in Nyasema's home. They would squeeze into the cramped adobe hut, cow dung collected on their bare feet from *ifanda*, the cow's path leading to the homestead. Their girlish giggles echoed all the way to *idemu*, forcing me to wish I had been born a girl! As the only boy among seven siblings, I had always tried to assert my presence in the women's hut. However, the girls, including my sisters, would summarily kick me out. "*Nyumba ya akhema*—women's houses are for women!" I was told. I would then leave in humiliation, retreating to the wall to eavesdrop on their girlish whispers. Albeit, even when I joined the other boys outside, I never ceased to wonder "What do girls talk about when they are just girls?"

A typical day in Nyasema's home began with a pair of these young villagers finding their way to her *müsee* (frontyard). Like baby ducks, they would huddle together, seeking their place on the dusty floor. The older ones carried their younger siblings on their backs, while the able-bodied ones walked, nibbling on *ikhokho* for breakfast. This was the leftover cornbread, which had hardened overnight in the cold, such that chewing it was akin to gnawing on the sole of an old shoe.

They joked around Nyasema's pierced nose and round tattoos on her ash-smeared cheeks. "*Bibi*" they called her, meaning grandmother. "Tell us another story," they pleaded, as Nyasema attempted to deflect their requests. She would then concoct a tale from the depths of her imagination, narrating it in a manner that little ears were almost unmovable in the adobe kitchen.

The setting is often imbued with the scents of the kitchen, a fragrant mix of savory and sweat that intermingles with the lingering odor of unwashed baby bottoms and the subtle hint of smoke. And when these scents are coupled with sweet melodies of their farts as little ribs try hard to control their laughter, even the most vibrant sunset can be postponed. I have heard these stories repeated over and over again, yet the mistress storyteller never recounted them in the same manner. Her renditions were so vivid that her listeners could almost reach out and touch the characters in the tales.

Thus, Nyasema never lacked for youthful companionship in her *makitra*. This was her way of enlisting the help of house workers to run errands, such as grinding millet for *magahi* drink or chopping firewood for *ugee wa ademi*—a cowherd's lunch.

"Look at her," she would sneer at the snotty child who seemed fascinated by the *idodiga* ring. "Do you really think this can be attained so easily? I am a woman, you fool," she added with a mixture of pride and discomfort. The girls around her would laugh, not taking her words seriously. "You young girls today—just look at her! You are all useless," she taunted the youngsters who lounged around her, begging for another story. "Tell us another one, bibi," they giggled. "Tell us about *imaa*," they teased. "*Imaa*? Do you think you can capture the lion?" She refused to tell them. And even when she attempted to, it was a complete extortion. No woman would ever reveal the mysteries of *imaa* to uncircumcised children. It was the women's rite of passage and the ultimate secret behind the power of womanhood.

Nyasema had converted from her traditional cultural beliefs to Christianity a few years ago. With a small cross attached to the traditional beaded necklace, which hung on her slender neck, and with a held half-torn Bible under her armpit, when that happened, she was a new woman beyond transformation. Since then, people said that she had changed, although the term "change" seemed overrated for a woman who had lived her entire life with traditional values. What did "change" mean, anyway?

Yes, she had stopped drinking *ntue*, the local beer that used to cause fights with my father. She attended church more often these days and sang in the women's choir. I suppose one could categorize her as an "active Christian" or "born-again Christian," as they say. However, those things did not define her as a woman. Nyasema, the woman I knew, the woman who appears in my dreams, was a riddle that came alive in folk tunes. Even today, though she may appear "new" in the Christian sense, I could still hear echoes of her old melodies, which lingered in her supposedly new faith.

Traditional women like Nyasema grew up with a deep sense of loyalty to their culture. They were born girls but raised to become women, and Nyasema was no exception. She would rather die than speak out against the woman inside her. The tradition that raised her was nothing like her new faith. Though her new religion did not permit her to practice her cultural customs, her heart and soul were still bound to them. If she had stopped taking part in those traditions, it was not necessarily because she was now a Christian. The colonial religion was merely a white mask that covered a black face, without ever explaining or changing the woman inside her.

She, like others of her upbringing, would rather remain silent than argue against things she held dear. Customs like *mahumo, ifaha, ihungu,* or female circumcision were sacrosanct. She would never insult them the way Europeanized girls did. To her, any uncircumcised woman, regardless of age, remained a "fool." They had not reached maturity in their womanhood. They have chosen to remain girls, nonexistent in the woman's world. They may have grown physically, but they remained immature in the ways of womanhood. My mother would never reveal her cultural knowledge to the "imprudent," as she called them. They were unclean and impure, incapable of understanding such purity.

She was a devout Christian, yet she refrained from denigrating her cultural traditions as "barbaric" or "old-fashioned" in modern parlance. My attempt to comprehend this enigmatic woman was an arduous task, requiring more than mere effort. On the surface, she appeared to be a simple embodiment of her culture, an individual, a solitary story that seemingly manifested in every unique form of being. However, her multifaceted nature brought forth the inherent duality of womanhood. If every woman is a story, then stories do not possess singularity. No story can be a lone story; every tale is part of a larger, interconnected narrative. Stories are not static, but instead resist being captured, fixed, or relegated to a singular identity. Yet stories, in their essence, do not just sit there: they seek freedom; they are not found but constructed.

My mother was such a woman, embodying two different personas within a single story. As I delved deeper into her past, she reminded me of how women in our culture were expected to speak less about their realities. "Secrets" were their strength, allowing them to maintain a façade of cheerfulness amidst inner turmoil. To comprehend such bravery, one would require speculation or insight from underneath lyrics of their labor songs, which captured fragments of their experiences—blending hope and lamentation.

Nyasema's songs, like those of many others, were infused with memories, encapsulating both social structures and cultural evolution. Through her music and graceful dance moves, we could discern traces of the past intermingled with modernity, evoking emotions of joy and sorrow simultaneously. "I will ask my dad," one song goes, "I will ask my mother about the creation—who created us? What person created this—this creation? The singular creation that is not the same! The creation for all to abide by." This lamentation questioned the creation of mankind, expressing the singularity and diversity that exists within it. As it was for her song, so Nyasema was a complicated piece of a performance—a product of her multifaceted identity.

As a teenager, Nyasema's passion for singing was evident, a skill she inherited from her mother. She then sent herself to a missionaries' school only to put herself in trouble with her father. Since then, her life took a new turn. She was forced to return home to become a woman. That was back when Tanzania was still Tanganyika—a British territory.

The coming of *uhuru* found her already complete with the song of freedom in her mouth. They even call her "Mama Uhuru," literally meaning "a freedom woman." Her elegant voice was a staple at cultural and political events. Whether it was at local beer gatherings, the *imaa* arena, or political rallies, Nyasema dominated the stage. Regardless of her reputation, when she sat down in the evening, when she was herself, she despised her missed past with comments such as "I could have reached very far."

Today, she often aids her failing eyesight with a pointing finger, casting a glance at her Bible's unadorned pages and lamenting, "if I had completed my education, I would have been able to read three times faster than I do now." On other days, she would observe young people returning home from school and remark, "Don't think I had a small brain like yours; I was quite intelligent." These statements were often followed by a retelling of her interrupted past.

I feel compelled to commit this fanciful narrative to paper. This piece of writing is solely an endeavor on my part to comprehend the intricacies of these emotions and pay tribute to the cherished memories they evoke. Encapsulated within this introspection are the stories of many, albeit a select few. My prose represents my personal recollection, an exploration of my shortcomings as a man trying to grasp the essence of femininity. The individuals for whom this tale is crafted have carried grins upon their visages, concealing the malevolence that lurks in the world beyond their tinted countenances. This is the chronicle of those who bear invisible wounds and tears that have likely dried upon their cheeks without notice.

Hughes' poignant words in "Harlem"[1] ring true, for the pain of "a dream deferred" is a weighty burden that can be difficult to shake off.

The story of women in our cultures, in Tanzania and across Africa, is a dream that has been "deferred" for too long. Retrieving a lost past is an impossible task. My goal is to remember it, confront its traumas, and rebuild its ethereal shapes. Thus, we embark on a journey of capturing the shadow through the lens of our modern, disabled eyes. We confront the complexities of incomprehensible, grappling with the harsh realities of the translucent forms of being, while simultaneously shining a light on the strength and resilience of women in Tanzanian cultures.

1. Hughes, "Harlem."

II

-

"If you are not dead, you are not formed"

—Swahili proverb

—

EVEN AFTER MORE THAN eighteen years, these memories have continued to haunt me: of a pregnant woman, half-naked, lying on the ground in her own feces and blood—DEAD. This remains the most unforgettable and tragic incident I have ever witnessed.

Those familiar with Igengu will concede that it is akin to an autonomous state. Yet, Igengu is a humble remote village, enshrouded in an aura of mystique. To outsiders, it is a place of invisibility where legal systems are rendered ineffectual. That was where my diocese had assigned me as a pastor. In Tanzania, a pastor does not enjoy the liberty of choosing a congregation; instead, the diocese assigns one. I arrived promptly, only a few months after an old woman was publicly caned to death, believed to be a sorceress. Intrigued, I sought to understand how the villagers had identified her as a sorceress. "Because her eyes were red," they replied. "Her eyes were red?" I repeated, as if I had not heard it.

Initially, the correlation between "red eyes" and sorcery was incomprehensible, at least from my Arimi cultural perspective. In a place where the smoke from burning millet stalks fills the air in every woman's kitchen, one would rather suffer from irritated eyes that have become red, watery, and itchy than be subjected to suspicion of being a sorceress. However, I reminded myself that the Arimi were one of 158 ethnic groups in Tanzania, and there was much to be learned.

Zahoro, a young man whom the congregation had placed in my care, became my cultural guide, explaining the obscure cultural cues and mysteries I had encountered. "It is that serious," he confirmed. "That's why Igengu is a witch-free village; they do not condone witches here," he explained. "Well! That is fine, but how can you be sure that someone is a witch?" I inquired earnestly. "Oh yes, the witches are unmistakable—just look at their eyes; they are red," he responded with conviction.

And so, I found myself embarking on a new and challenging role, one that would test my cultural understanding in ways I never could have imagined. My journey had just begun. Inexperienced as I was, I fastened myself for a pastoral role like a naive apprentice, embarking on a new dance. And I was determined to rise to the challenge in this mysterious and complex Tanzanian village.

From the surrounding villages, Igengu evoked mixed reactions among the people. Some lauded it as a "village of no-nonsense," while others admonished, "go there only if you are ready to surrender your life." When word got around that I was being posted to work in Igengu, a fellow pastor had remarked with incredulity, "it seems like the church leadership doesn't hold you in high regard. Why else would they send you to Igengu?" To which I responded with a query of my own: "And why not Igengu?" It was an answer I would come to regret.

At first glance, as I arrived in a rented aging Landcruiser, Igengu appeared to be a typical dusty hamlet. I had grown up in a village myself and had lived in conditions that were harsher than this. I couldn't fathom what could make life unbearable here. Fresh out of theological training, brimming with zeal and enthusiasm, I was a young, unmarried man ready for the adventure that lay ahead—or so I thought.

Issa, the driver who had ferried me to the village, had seemed incredulous at the acceptance of my post. "Kaghondi!" he exclaimed, "this place is situated in the midst of nowhere! Are you certain that you want me to drop you off here?" he had asked, as if he had a choice to take me back. I chortled nonchalantly, not out of apathy but because I had already arrived. "No worries, Issa," I rejoined jocularly, "I will be just fine." I was oblivious to the weight of my call.

Issa handed me my half-full suitcase, which contained only a few items of clothing, since that was all I had. To create the impression that it was fuller, I had included a few items as padding, such as cornflour for the first month, some books, and a charcoal stove. What else would a bachelor pastor need at the start of his career? However, before I could take hold of it, a throng of villagers who had swarmed the vehicle grabbed it hastily to welcome their pastor. Issa bid me farewell with a fake smile and then drove back to Singida. Little did I know that it was to be the last time we would see each other, as fate had other plans for him.

Nestled amidst a scorching stream in the sinuous valleys of central Tanzania, Igengu is a place of unrelenting heat and suffocating humidity. Its luscious soil, a covetable shade of ebony, appears to be incredibly fertile, yet it tends to dry out quickly due to the unreliable rainfall, creating a murky cloud of dust that has a knack for soiling white garments. This rich soil is only a thin layer atop a harsh sheet of gravel, contributing to its unforgiving nature.

It seems that the soil in Igengu is never quite satisfied with moisture. When it rains, the village's narrow cow paths are transformed into surging streams, and the entire village appears to sink like a bog. But only two days later, the searing heat from the rift valley beats down upon the ground with unrelenting ferocity, and the muddy pathways return to their arid state as if the village had not seen rain in years. Astonishingly, the locals are accustomed to this. They are only exasperated with the impenetrable earth when someone passes away. For that all the men in the village, including schoolboys, must take turns digging into the gravel bed to retrieve at least a few inches of soil for the burial. One cannot help but wonder how deep the toilet pits are in Igengu.

Mornings in Igengu greet one with an unyielding sun, whose heat stands still—swallowing all the hot air in its path, making it nearly impossible to breathe. The humidity is so oppressive that life inside the house feels like being trapped in a tunnel. Outside, the desert rages on with relentless fury, where even trees have relinquished their futile attempts at offering their shade. I had brought a charcoal stove with me, but it appeared to be of no use. The air here is stagnant, and starting a fire requires the skills of a seasoned fire-maker. However, somehow, this void, semi-desert, rugged, dark landscape has lured in many people, the majority of whom are multilingual ethnic groups.

Nyiramba and Nyisanzu were the dominant ethnic groups living side by side harmoniously. Nonetheless, the Sukuma and Barbaig communities added a kaleidoscope of cultural diversity to the melting pot of customs and traditions that are otherwise far apart. Interestingly, both groups were fluent in each other's dialects. Religion-wise, most villagers shunned mainstream religions like Christianity or Islam, opting instead for a non-conformist approach to spirituality. Despite this, a few small churches could be found within the vicinity of my congregation.

The staple food of the village was sorghum, complemented by other crops such as sunflower, groundnuts, and the popular sweet potatoes. During harvest time, most children would temporarily drop out of school to assist their parents in preserving the potatoes. Girls, on the other hand, would be seen moving in groups, walking on foot to Kinankamba, a hilly terrain, to collect firewood. These logs of wood were used to boil the sliced potatoes, known as *matoloa*, which would then be kept for the summer as a backup in case the sorghum crops failed due to the drought.

Collecting firewood was a task delegated to women and children, while the men would congregate in local bars or engage in hunting expeditions in the wilderness. Those who were lucky enough to find wild game would return home with a slice of meat hanging on their shoulders, but these days, deforestation has reduced such stories to mere folklore. Villagers reminisce about the days when deer were abundant, realizing that climate change is a stark reality that, if not mitigated, will rob future generations of the bounty that the land once offered.

Despite the cultural blend of Nyiramba and Nyisanzu, the peaceful coexistence between the ethnic groups was often disrupted by inter-ethnic conflicts. Often, tensions between the Barbaig and Sukuma groups simmered beneath the surface, with each party blaming the other. Two groups were particularly known for their ongoing animosity, with each group blaming the other for their misfortunes. The Barbaig people accused the Sukuma of encroaching on their forest and keeping massive cows that ruined their land. The Sukuma, in turn, accused the Barbaig of stealing their cows, leading to a decade-long conflict. The Barbaig, who were skilled in spear fighting, would often strike in the dead of night, stealing Sukuma's cows and accusing them of trespassing. The Sukuma warriors, in turn, would seek revenge, ambushing the Barbaig in the mountains to rescue their cows. The cycle of violence would continue, with the defeated party seething with rage and contemplating their next move.

Every time the Sukuma recaptured their stolen cows, they would seize all the bovines they could find, including those originally belonging to the Barbaig. This would provide the Barbaig with a pretext to return and retake "their cows." However, when the Barbaig invaded the Sukuma area to re-claim their cattle, they never separated them from the herds belonging to the Sukuma. They would sweep up all the cows that they could find. And so, the conflict never abated. Many men have been killed, with each ethnic group claiming to fight for "their" cows or "their" land to the point where it became difficult to ascertain which cows or lands belonged to which group.

For politicians, Igengu was nothing but a voting "gold mine"; at least, that was how I perceived it. Candidates, most of whom were running for a parliamentary seat, would only visit Igengu during their campaigns. They would come to Igengu to woo the villagers with hollow speeches, make false promises, and bribe the illiterate populace with local beers until they were drunk and oblivious to the value of their votes. The one who knew how to throw the best beer parties was considered "the man."

A drunken voter is as loyal as an ignorant one. On the day of the elec-tion, men wearing colorful hats would wake up with hangovers, donning the candidate's logo on their huts as if to obscure their muddled minds. Women, who were almost married to the candidate, would wear the gifted Khangas with the candidate's headstamp inscribed between their almost pant-less butts. That was the level of intimacy that ignorance and pov-erty could provide. They would vote to repay the debt for their beers and Khangas. This has always been the way. After every election, the people of Igengu would almost forget all their memories of the previous elections. They would only see the candidates again during the next election. And yet, they would vote for the same person, even when he had not fulfilled a single promise. Year after year, Igengu has remained the same, and this is true for most parts of the country.

Igengu is a destitute community, lacking even the most basic ameni-ties. Something like a road wide enough for a car or a pharmacy to ob-tain a malaria pill. Access to electricity and a decent education are distant dreams. Despite this harsh reality, the incumbent member of parliament, in a shocking display of arrogance and corruption, once gave an interview where he referred to his constituents as "chickens." To him, the mere sound of "grains"—the term he used for bribes—was enough to lure these "chick-ens" into giving him their votes. And for more than twenty five years, this trick has proved him right.

This interview took place shortly after he gifted a soccer ball and twelve sets of outfits to the local team—a well-known tactic of Tanzanian politicians to woo young voters. As there were not enough presents for all the teams in the village, they had to compete against each other to win the coveted prize. To the young people of Igengu, who had never before possessed real soccer equipment, this MP was seen as a "man of the people," caring about their welfare. But in reality, he viewed them as brainless creatures, easily manipulated by the sound of his bribes.

As a result, the youth of Igengu formed local soccer teams to compete for the "MP's Cup." The game lasted two weeks and culminated in a disaster. Several young men were seriously injured, and there was significant property damage beyond the soccer field. But I may be getting ahead of myself.

****

It was the house where I resided that allowed me to comprehend Igengu more profoundly. Let me clarify. This single-room hut with a dusty floor and no toilet was the best abode in the village. Its walls were constructed of adobe bricks and its roof was made of rusty iron, half attached and half held down by hefty rocks. If one of those boulders were to come loose while I was slumbering, I would not have lived to write this account. "What a better way to perish," I pondered on occasion during sleepless nights, imagining the decayed roof collapsing onto my face and severing my head from my body. What a misfortune it would be for my mother to lose her only son.

Lying in bed, I could gaze up at the roof at night, which was, in a sense, a metal rag where its naked holes mixed with bright stars to cast their spotlights on my bed. Now and then, a winter cloud would provide some covering, obstructing the direct light from the stars. But when it rained, the murky soil that had collected on top of the roof for the entire summer would be rinsed away and sent cascading onto my bedclothes. In a few months, my once-favorite pastoral bed linens had been transformed into unrecognizable scraps of cloth.

But as Arimi's wisdom always reminded me, *tye tye mbee uvaya ubahu*—something obnoxious is better than nothing." This hut, which had withstood the heat of the rift valley, was better than anything else in the village that resembled it in any way. And like in any other situations, "time" has its ways of rendering our conception of reality neutral. Time passed. As it passed, everything eventually started to look indistinguishably normal— from a hut's insecurity to the pandemonium in the village.

The hut was rented from a young man who "had been to the city." Somehow, those who have "traveled to the city" did not return empty-handed, as the villagers would say. *"Ametoka mjini"*—he has been to the

11

city—people would whisper about a person like this young man. His name was Yesaya, the son of Senga—one of the church elders in the congregation that I led. Most young men like Yesaya often dropped out of school and "ran" to the city "*kutafuta maisha*"—to seek their fortunes. Boys have more advantages than girls in these ventures. While boys would engage in tough jobs that they could find in the city, girls would often endure unpaid babysitting work, most of whom would end up trading their girlhood for a morsel of bread.

Thus, many girls face immeasurable atrocities. Even if they regretted it later, there was little chance they could escape those harsh environments. They were frequently locked up in the house by their inhumane bosses before they could find their way home. Even those who made it back would still lose themselves in trying to accumulate enough money for bus fare. Those who were fortunate enough to return safely were perhaps pregnant or already with "fruits" of that sort from "who knows what man?"

The rise of cosmopolitanism in Tanzania, therefore, marked the emergence of "children of the city." These will grow up without knowledge of their fathers. This, of course, unless HIV-AIDS was involved.

As these young men and women arrived in the village, they concealed the truth of their city's plight. Despite the hardships they encountered, they maintained a sophisticated demeanor that exuded modernity and attracted the attention of impressionable rural youth. Girls would resort to skin-bleaching and makeup application to appear lighter and softer, while the boys donned neckties and white sandals, pretending to be money-mongers.

Yesaya, the owner of the house where I currently resided, was one of those young men whom Arimi called "a gentle Well is what drowns." Like a male hyena who never asked to attend the feast, Yesaya had probably fucked every girl of his liking in Igengu. His house, where I was currently accommodating my pastoral holiness, was where everything happened. Imagine girls who were used to being laid in the sugar cane farms, being given a chance to rub their backs on a mattress for the first time.

The house was in an ideal location, neither close to the village center for people to see who comes in and out, nor far from other residents. It was a perfect place for girls to sneak in and out without being noticed by their parents. What happened inside there would prove that if humans were genes' ways of making more genes, then cities were people's ways of making more people. And the city had transformed Yesaya to more than a favorable gene in Igengu.

There was something else about the house that I needed to decipher. Over time, I had noticed that not a single day would pass without a stranger, most of whom were men, stopping by. Every time they reached the house, they would ask for something they called "*dawa*"—"medicine." Some asked for what they called "business." "What business?" I always asked, but they would not answer me and would leave. There was something very strange in these conversations, I thought, that I could not make sense of. What could they be asking for? I was not a doctor to prescribe any "*dawa*"—what was all this about? Over time, most of them learned quickly that the owner of the house was no longer residing there. "Where is the owner of the house?" I remember some asking. Soon or later, they started avoiding stopping by, and a few who visited would leave without further explanation.

It made me wonder what I was missing in these conversations. I could not help but becoming curious about why these strangers always asked similar questions. Obviously, every group has its own implicit language, and as for me, they probably wondered, "Who the hell is this dude?"

Zahoro, my house helper, was the one who unmasked the secret: "Oh! They are asking for marijuana," he said. "Yesaya, the owner of the house, used to sell them marijuana." I could not believe it. "Marijuana—in a pastor's house?" I exclaimed, forgetting that it was a rental house. I would later realize that marijuana was unbelievably common in Igengu. This was merely a plant that did not grow by accident on people's farms. In Tanzania, marijuana is illegal, but in Igengu, people would likely "boycott" if asked to stop growing it. What police officer had the guts to come to Igengu anyway? Did I not say that Igengu was like its own country state? It was an astonishing realization, how in the village such like this, laws meant nothing.

****

Music was the only means through which I could make friends. I needed to bridge the gap between myself and the youth, and music seemed to be the perfect way to achieve this. I decided to introduce beginner jam sessions, and these quickly gained popularity. We held them twice a week, usually after dinner, at my house. Timing was always a challenge, and we started rehearsals when we had enough people with instruments.

The village youth, many of whom sang in the church choir, responded enthusiastically. Igengu, like many choir groups in Tanzania, were fascinated by modern instruments, and choirs would buy or carve them even if they had no idea how to use them. With my passion for music, I introduced electric guitar, bass, and keyboard lessons. The sessions were fun and engaging.

After a few months, the sounds of locally made and amplified electric instruments blended with traditional shakers. The sound was so captivating that it drew almost the entire village to the pastor's yard. We transformed bicycle brakes into guitar strings, and once a dead FM boombox was engineered into a powered amplifier. We refurbished the junk to herald the good news to an abandoned village. A fascinating, jazzy sound was produced from overloaded speakers that probably complained of the dead batteries. Poor but unique sounds kept young people always asking "When are we meeting again next week?" With this equipment, much of which was made from recycled electronics, we had proven how only motivation was enough to push the edge of technology

Every day overtook the day before it. As days passed, rehearsals began to attract neighboring choir groups, who wanted to take music lessons from us. We went from using cell batteries to a diesel generator, which required a journey of almost fifty miles to buy if we had enough funds. Most of our members had to sell chicken eggs to contribute. But with the diesel generator, we could not only power our amplifier, but we could also connect electrical bulbs to help us see our fingers as they chased down unwritten musical notes on the hand-chiseled guitars.

People in the village didn't read music. It all depended on the power of memorization. We would play the same patterns over and over again until each musician mastered their part, from the melodic structure and harmony to the orchestration and progression. If someone missed a rehearsal or forgot their part, we would have to start over, but this often led to surprising improvements.

Despite the challenges, we learned to embrace the process of recreating musical ideas until they took concrete shape as a performable piece. The product was not as important as the journey we took to get there. Watching each musician grow from struggling with finger placement to producing recognizable melodies was rewarding. And seeing them create something of their own was astonishing.

What was more meaningful than the joy of discovery? Above all, we were gathered by church music, and it was music that brought us together in ways that surpassed any religious denomination. Music had become our religion, and we worshiped it with all our hearts. After all—is music not the last religion on earth? I believe that when the religion has faded out on the earth's surface, music will remain as the last goddess.

****

Days in Igengu lack the exceptional variety one might find in more picturesque locales. The mornings do not commence with the reddish hue of hilltop skies or the soft glow behind yellow lilies. There are no joyous warblers or melodious songs of honeybees. No blooms of scented flowers or harmonious azure water streams. The village is situated in a semi-desert region, and the monotonous vista of its arid landscape constitutes its sole adornment.

In its essence, the village embodies a sense of profound pessimism that obscures any traces of ecstasy. It exudes the stale air of yesteryear and the redolence of dust, devoid of all singing creatures except for crickets and morning roosters, whose crows herald the arrival of each day.

Afternoons are arrhythmic and lack meaning. The relentless sun beats down without inspiring any industrious ants to build anthills or creative artists to envision ingenious works. The arid evenings are as unromantic as the people who inhabit them, and the sunset fails to cast its radiance behind the shades of trees. Instead, it expires unceremoniously across the ridges, leaving the nightfall bereft of any contrast to the preceding morning or afternoon.

Thus, every day is merely a day, with good days uncelebrated by any sense of accomplishment and bad days distinguished solely by their utter chaos. On one such typical Tuesday in Igengu, however, the sunset altered everything. I had arranged the instruments outside my house for the evening rehearsal and was awaiting the arrival of my musicians when a young man forcefully entered my yard.

"Pastor!" he exclaimed breathlessly. "You need to see this! Shamakota is killing his wife!"

The young man, Simon, was one of members of the music group, but he was too winded to convey the details of the situation. The weight of his words stunned me into momentary numbness, and I dropped the sound cable from my hands. But my senses quickly returned, and I leapt over the musical instruments to run towards Shamakota's house.

I wasn't entirely sure what I hoped to accomplish at that moment, but I knew that I had to act. The pitch-black sky cloaked the agricultural path ahead of us, foretelling the darkness that would follow that ominous

Tuesday. Simon and I raced towards the unknown, with the premonitory raincloud transforming into a thunderstorm, and the rhythmic lightning illuminating the treacherous terrain of the village. Only the gods knew what lay beneath our pounding feet.

As we continued to run towards Shamakota's house on the eastern side, I began to fall behind while Simon's figure growing increasingly indistinct in the distance. "If I can just get there," I thought to myself, but my chest felt as though it was exploding with the effort, and I desperately needed to catch my breath.

A few moments later, Simon had disappeared altogether, but I continued to push myself beyond my limits, relying solely on my instincts to guide me through the night. When I arrived at the scene, the area was surrounded by dozens of people, but an eerie silence hung in the air. Gasping for air like a defeated boxer, I forced my way through the crowd to the heart of the horrifying scene. Some recognized me and parted to allow the pastor access to the incident.

From the dark shadows, Nikota lay motionless on the ground. With trepidation, I approaching her. I kneeled beside her body and lifted her left arm towards me. She displayed no visible signs of injury, yet, the woman laid too peacefully to be true. On the ground, her eyes had closed and her mouth agape in a manner that forced itself into my mega memory. A pool of vomit and blood stained the ground beside her, an eerie contrast to the quiet stillness of the scene.

As I strained to assess her condition in the dim light, a sense of foreboding washed over me. Was this all just a terrible dream? The expectant gazes of the surrounding onlookers only added to the sense of mounting pressure, as though they were waiting for Jesus to perform some miraculous feat through my confusion. Desperate to help, I tried to roll Nikota over onto her back, but a chill ran down my spine as I felt the lack of warmth emanating from her body. "How can this be true?" I muttered to myself, my heart heavy with a sense of loss.

The scene unfolded with dizzying speed. The shock had taken hold of the crowd, and I was left feeling helpless as I searched for someone to explain what had happened. But all I heard were murmurs and the sound of women crying. I placed my index finger on Nikota's neck, hoping to feel her pulse, but there was none. I stretched her arm out again as if to will her back to life. "Stand up, Nikota. Please, stand up!" I begged her. But the response I received was that of a body that had surrendered its fight. Nikota was irrevocable. She was dead.

I remained on my knees, taking in the rare breath of my life. I never knew that death could come so suddenly, that life could be so fragile. I never recognized the meaning of life. Now I understood it, through a woman that I did not even know enough to trace my memories of her.

Nikota, a six-months pregnant woman, had been killed. She had been beaten like a wild cat, her abdomen stamped upon by her drunken husband. After unimaginable torture, her soul had given in to earthly pains and surrendered to the desire for a release from this world. A beautiful, dark-chocolate-skinned woman with a pure heart was gone. She had been sent too quickly to the afterlife, where no one complains of innocence. I wondered if she was happy in heaven, if such a place existed, and if she had found the rest she deserved. Sadly, I later learned that her own two-year-old daughter had suffered a similar fate at the hands of the same man a few years prior. Nikota had now joined her daughter, leaving behind two beautiful girls who had yet to find their place in a world that cared little for women.

I overheard a woman grieving on the left side of the crowd: "He is that way." Her voice trembled with sadness. 'Three years ago, he murdered his two-year-old daughter and ran away . . . now his wife," she added, her tone laced with anguish. Another woman nearby wept and directed her anger towards the men in the crowd who seemed to know the whereabouts of the murderer but had taken no action. "He will come back to kill each one of us. That's what you're all waiting for," she cried. A third woman chimed in, "They do nothing, thinking he will disappear forever," while another lamented, "They know well that he ran to deceive our memories." By "they," she meant the accomplices—the men.

I struggled to comprehend what had just occurred. How could someone's life be so recklessly taken? I looked up at the sky, feeling defeated and thinking, "God, do you really witness these atrocities?" There was no response from the heavens, only the dimming stars, fading amidst what seemed like a premature rain. "What a brutal death," I muttered angrily, distancing myself from the corpse.

It was at that moment that I suddenly came to my senses: "Where the hell am I?" What village is this? I couldn't call the police as there were no stations nearby, nor could I make any phone calls since there were no phones. All the sudden, the words of Issa, the driver, echoed in my ears,

"This village is in the middle of nowhere." Now I could understand what he meant, thinking, "what had brought me here in the first place?"

The next day, Nikota was buried, just like any other woman who died a normal death. Since she was not a member of my church, I was not in charge of her burial. However, I attended the service that was held as part of the community, standing at the back of the burial place, behind the huge crowd that had gathered around the extended area of tombs. As I listened to the preacher's words, memories of my childhood came flooding back to me. I recalled phrases like "He is a man, and you were born a girl" that had made no sense to me all these years.

The preacher seemed more heartbroken than I was. He preached as though he were speaking directly to the deceased, altering his words to suit the occasion. We all had to listen and find ourselves in the midst of his sermon. "My daughter," he called Nikota, even though she was now just a wrapped-up body. "This man has taken you from us because you couldn't fight back. He did this because he is a man, and you are a woman. This is what he thought you deserved—after all you've done for him. Because he knew you would not fight back, right? The man whom you loved and married. The man you gave birth to his children. This man whom you served food every morning and evening. What kind of a coward is he? Who repays the women in his life with such cruelty?"

The preacher lamented at length, speaking with such intensity that it was as if tears were streaming down his face. Clutching his Bible and hymn book in his left hand, he scooped the soil from the side of the tomb. With an air of unease, he spoke words of farewell: "Go in peace, daughter of the Lord. May your suffering fight on your behalf." The men, myself included, began to cover the tomb with earth until it formed a hill, a silent testament to Nikota's hidden courage. Slowly, and one by one, people began to leave the graveyard, walking quietly to their homes. Nikota had found her final resting place.

As we departed, the heavy rain that had evaded us the night before began to form. A ripening cloud that had nearly dissipated suddenly matured, and rain poured down in torrents as if to wash away our sorrow. "It has washed away the curse," the villagers later remarked.

Following tradition, the people of the village gathered at Nikota's home to mourn. However, Shamakota was still nowhere to be found, and no search was launched. Rumors began to circulate that he was still hiding in the village, yet no police report was filed, and no search warrant was issued. In short, this was a cold-blooded case that did not exist in the eyes of the law.

Later that week, the family performed customary rituals to "cleanse the house from the curse." This involved sacrificing a goat and sprinkling its blood and *ufuu* around the house and tomb. Once the ritual was complete, people returned to their homes, and the village went back to normal as if nothing had ever happened.

III

-

"If you don't know how to die, visit the graveyard"

—Swahili proverb

—

THE CHURCH BUILDING WHERE I ministered was a dilapidated hall constructed from mud, and its roof comprised interwoven branches covered in clay. The weight of the roof was borne by several robust V-shaped pillars placed in the aisle between two rows of brick pews, one on either side. The aisle was the sole means of entry and exit, save for the front-facing aperture intended for the clergy and their assistants. However, during regular worship services, the pastor and his assistants would process in through the rear door after adorning their vestments in the corner outside the building, as no church office was available.

Both doors and windows were mere uncovered openings in the adobe wall. When the building was unoccupied, particularly during the week, children in the vicinity found solace in this space to relieve themselves. Were it not for the women responsible for Sunday mornings, the service would take place amid the stench of human waste. To mitigate the malodorous conditions, the floor had to be frequently watered to lessen the rank odor and swirling dust.

Notwithstanding the floor being watered, in the dry season, the unprotected windows permitted all manner of earthly dust to enter the hall. When this dust settled on worshippers' faces, a homemade lotion became an adhesive, leaving only their teeth visible amidst the cemented dark earth. The rainy season was no better, as the water seeped through the roof's less adherent clay, causing it to drip onto the worshipers' shoulders. The church altar's décor had become unrecognizable over time. Sometimes, the service had to be interrupted until the rain subsided. Nevertheless, God's presence was so palpable within these walls that these minor destructible elements were negligible, serving as a reminder that the church is the embodiment of God's imperfect work. Despite the inclement weather, people attended the worship services in droves. This was my first congregation as a pastor, and it held a special place in my heart.

A momentous occasion had arrived: Angela, a young woman whom I had only just met in the choir, was getting married. Weddings are special events in Igengu, as they are in many places in Tanzania. This particular wedding was even more special to me. On the one hand, Angela and Zahoro were siblings, and since Zahoro lived with me, their entire family had become my friends. But more importantly, this was my first wedding as a pastor to solemnize. I recall standing on a rickety wooden pulpit, which threatened to collapse due to its corroded nails. The pulpit required repair, but even a single nail was too costly to afford. The congregation's offerings were redirected towards the "parsonage rent," which was TZS 10,000 ($5) at the time. Yet, even this meager sum was difficult to attain.

The church collected a mere TZS 20,000 ($10) per month, most of which had to be sent to the diocese, with the remainder divided between my salary, the house rent, staff salaries, and other congregational services, such as bread and wine for the holy communion. One can only wonder how much money was left to cover these expenses. But that is a discussion for another day.

In my rumpled pastoral robes, I stood ready to unite two young couples in a supposedly everlasting bond. Love, I thought, is the strangest of things, yet I knew it was an emotion that defies logic. This day had begun with mixed emotions like any other wedding. For at least a month, people had been feasting and dancing day and night in anticipation of the final ceremony. Some had lost their voices from excessive singing and revelry.

At the church, the service began with a procession. The groom entered first, accompanied by his best man and the sounds of throbbing drums from his side of the relatives. An hour later, the bride processed in with her company. Both sides had invited their distant friends and relatives, although this did not apply to villagers and neighbors who would come anyway. The building was packed with people who had arrived two hours before the service. The singing of traditional songs, women's ululations, and dances entertained all corners of the neighborhood. Christians and non-Christians alike were present, whether invited or not.

This particular tradition has something great that must be said about it. As the bride processed in, her side of the relatives danced around her while blocking the narrow aisle to slow her down. "Why in a hurry? Your husband is not your kinsman," they would tease the bride. At the same time, the groom's side would try to push them out of the way, claiming "it is too late; she is already ours." This was all part of teasing and celebration, a form of a musical-dance-full argument, if you will.

From the outside, the scene looked like a fight or some kind of competition, especially between siblings and their counterparts. It was *mchezo wa mashemaji*. Each group would try to do the opposite of the other. For example, Angela's siblings tried to stop her from moving until the groom's siblings paid them some tokens called *kinanzala* as a gesture of appreciation. They had to pay if they wanted the bride to move an inch. Otherwise, there would be no procession or service. If the groom's side was not brave enough to overcome those barriers, they would find themselves paying a lot of *kinanzala*, and the bride would only move a few steps before being stopped again. At this point, the wedding service could be paused for hours.

As a cultural outsider in Igengu, this was something amazing to watch, as long as it did not turn into a real fight. A pastor had no say in this game but to wait until groups came to some agreements. This was supposed to be a jocular traditional game, although some people would get offended, especially from the groom's side. These emotions were part of it, testing each other's limits of aggression, patience, and bravery.

After each side had tested their strengths and bravery against each other, the bride was let go. As she walked to the front, two groups of singers and dancers continued to compete through songs. For Angela, these songs were sung side by side by both groups, as if they were in a conversation. The other group sang something of a challenge for another group to respond to. These songs might not be easy to grasp at first. Their messages were sometimes hidden, and some people might laugh while others weep. Somehow, through songs, I concluded that joy and sorrow were not necessarily far apart from each other.

The melody emanating from Angela's siblings held a mournful tone. The lead vocalist, with a resplendent timbre, intoned, "*Mwana ng'ombe wasita masunsu*—My calf has refused her mother's nipples. A calf has spat her mother's milk." The chorus responded, "Yes! My calf has jumped off the *kraal*." Accompanied by the traditional dance, women swayed their bodies, bouncing imaginary babies on their backs. The lyrics portrayed Angela as the "calf" who had renounced her mother's nourishment, indicating her desire for independence from her family.

As the celebration progressed, Angela's kin joined the dance, encircling her, a throng that included her aunties, sisters, uncles, friends, and more. Angela's mother, with a drum clasped firmly between her thighs, she wistfully played a steady rhythm, while another person struck the gong made of cow horn, and some jingled bells on their feet. When whistles and shouting were added to the cacophony, the event's emotional tenor vacillated between a farewell and a celebration, confounding onlookers like me.

The song from the groom's side was in sharp contrast to the previous one—filled with paradox and humor. The women's ululations from this group echoed, surpassing the low-hanging muddy roof. With their tongues wagging furiously, they howled triumphantly, seemingly confirming that those who bore male children were always on the winning side. The song was directed at both the bride and her parents. "They traded you for a goat," the lead singer announced. "Yes! They traded you for goats," the chorus replied. "Look at your covetous parents! They sold you for cows?" the group continued to jest. "Yes, indeed, they did—because they knew she was obstinate—isn't that right?" The leader's lyrics became more pronounced. "She was not easy to keep—ha! That's why they had to let her come to us," the group rejoined. "It's alright, though! We are people of benevolence and compassion. We agreed to shoulder your 'burden,'" the song persisted.

As I contemplated these songs, I mused, "If they were meant to be humorous, their lyrics were incredibly amusing. But what if they were real? How could one differentiate between jest and sincerity?" To me, the entire celebration was a frustrating conversation, particularly if one was uninitiated in the culture.

****

As I observed Angela, I couldn't help but notice her sobriety. Her bridesmaid was struggling to keep up with her tearful face as the makeup had given up on its worthiness, unable to withstand the wave of tearful emotion that had washed over her beauty. The sight of her tears made me think back to my home village and a memory from my teenage years, when my uncle's daughter, Fatuma, got married.

Fatuma was the only daughter of Makasi Nkami, born between two boys: Igwe, the firstborn, and Mahanju, the youngest. As is customary in many Tanzanian cultures, boys are prepared to succeed their fathers, while girls are expected to marry. Before Fatuma even knew she was ready for marriage, her father had already received a marriage proposal from a complete stranger, a man she didn't even know.

As a young boy, I found the whole process awkward, but I kept my questions to myself until my mother explained it to me years later. According to her, Fatuma was married to a man whose age tripled hers, and she became his second wife even though his daughters were almost her age. My mother explained that there were two reasons why Fatuma's parents agreed to this marriage.

The first reason was that the man wanted another wife because his first wife had no male children. If a woman doesn't bear a male child, it is common for a man to take another wife, but this often depends on the man himself. The second reason was that the man was wealthy, owning many cows. Fatuma's brother, Igwe, was greedy and wanted many cows as the bride price. My mother confided in me that if Fatuma had disagreed with the marriage arrangements, Igwe would have killed her.

The words of my mother went straight to my heart, and I remember asking her why nobody tried to help Fatuma. Her response was simply, "*Mwanangu, kua uyaone*"—My son, grow up to observe things for yourself. Even as a teenager, I could not fathom why one's future should be dictated like this, but I had to accept that this was the reality of our culture.

Fatuma's wedding was not held in a church, as she was a Muslim. However, her tears made me wonder whether Angela's tears were the same. The only difference was that Angela's wedding was consensual, at least from the church's perspective, although certain moments made me question her decisions. How could her tears be any different from those of my cousin? I could not come to a straightforward conclusion. To me, both of their weeping, when blended with the throb of the drums, created a complex emotional atmosphere in what was a translucent cultural space. Was this a joyful weeping?

Mom had told me that Fatuma did not shed a single tear during initiation, not even when she faced a "lion" during *Imaa*. Supposedly, she was a courageous girl who was determined to realize her full potential. She attended school with my other sisters and shared their passion for further-ing their education. Unfortunately, Fatuma was caught in the middle of "old-new" cultural transitions.

The only difference was that, while Angela stopped weeping after we sat down in the church, Fatuma cried throughout the entire wedding. I knew that Fatuma's tears were tears of resistance and not joy. Her percep-tion of life and expectations were not aligned with her parents. But could she change the situation? Could she stand up against the cultural roots that had raised her this far?

Whatever her opinion was, Fatuma was to get married—a wedding of tears and "no choice." Eventually, she had to weigh her teenage years against her loyalty to the family. At the top of it all was the tradition that gave a woman little choice but to get married. People said that only "time" would change a married woman and transform her unwillingness into acceptance. Over time, when life becomes reality, her dreams of the future would be-come "reality." And that reality would mean accepting the fact that she has become a wife and has her own home. After all, among the many things a person needs to sustain marriage, "love" was perhaps the least significant for a cultural woman—obedience to her husband was.

Whether "love" has something to do with a person's emotions or it is just a human-made concept, to Fatuma, it has never existed. I sometimes wonder if "love" is innate or if it is simply imposed as life goes on. Women like Fatuma get married not because they "love" but when the time comes to be married. They are married because what else would a woman do? Marriage is what makes them women—have children and get over those cultural-social pressures.

Even in Tanzania as a whole, when people talk about the concept of marriage, it is discussed as a masculine process. Men are the ones who "marry." They are responsible for finding a woman. But women are "mar-ried." That has always been the case. Men in Tanzania/Africa "marry," and women are "married." The word "married" even in Swahili language cannot be applied to men.

The implication is that men are always active doers in the act of mar-rying, while women are passive—sometimes objectified in that passivity. That is the distinct vocabulary in Kiswahili between "marry" (kuoa) and "married" (kuolewa). Women are "married." Fatuma was "married."

In Tanzania, the societal expectations placed on women are noth-ing short of suffocating. The pressure to be married and bear children, particularly male children, is immense, leaving many women feeling as though their worth is only determined by their reproductive capabilities. This culture of gender bias is not just harmful; it is downright oppressive, as women are forced to endure the painful consequences of not meeting their husband's expectations.

Growing up in Arimi, I witnessed this injustice firsthand. I heard countless stories of men blaming their wives for not producing male children, treating them as mere baby-making machines instead of equal partners in their marriage. It was heart-wrenching knowing that my own mother had been a victim of this mentality, as she suffered under the weight of cultural expectations that deemed her unworthy due to her inability to bear a son.

The abuse that my mother endured was unimaginable, and it's no surprise that many women resort to desperate measures to try and conceive a son. However, the risks involved in this quest for a male heir are steep, as doubts about the paternity of a child can quickly tear a family apart. It's tragic that some women feel they have no other option but to resort to such tactics, all because of the gender bias ingrained in the cultural mindset.

The traditional option of a husband taking a second wife only perpetuates this cycle of oppression, as it creates a toxic environment where women are pitted against one another in a competition for their husband's affection. The concept of a "*mke mdogo*"—junior wife—is nothing short of abhorrent, as it forces women to navigate the complexities of polygamous marriage and often leads to unnecessary drama and heartbreak.

It's no wonder that women like Fatuma are left feeling exhausted and depleted, having given birth to multiple children in quick succession while trying to navigate the complexities of polygamous marriage. The toll that this lifestyle takes on women is evident in the rapid aging of their physical appearance, as they are forced to live their lives in a state of constant stress and anxiety.

Childbearing would not have been an insurmountable hurdle if joy and health permeated Fatuma's life and marriage. Yet, something far more insidious and corrosive had taken hold of her. "What could be the source of her misery?" I silently pondered. Departing my village to pursue my studies, I later returned during a break, only to hear that Fatuma was severely ill, having fled her husband's home to take refuge with her parents. At my uncle's house, I encountered a hollow shell of a woman, gaunt and despondent, unable to converse as she once did. Her spirit was crushed, the vitality in her eyes replaced with the bleakness of despair.

My mother later informed me that Fatuma was ill-treated by her husband and in-laws, forced to endure a life of servitude akin to that of a slave. Her marriage had transformed her into a hapless victim, robbed of her freedom, her dignity, and her very identity of womanhood. "I want to come home" she had insisted, as she sought escape from the purgatory of her existence, only to be rebuffed by the antiquated views of her kin, for whom the sanctity of marriage and the value of cattle outweighed the lives of their loved ones. "I want to come home" she cried, as if she was not already home. "Marriage is not easy" she was told by her mother.

Her marriage never transcended the material; thus Fatuma's family failed to grasp the urgency of her situation. Divorce, an unthinkable act of shame, threatened to tarnish the family's reputation, pushing Fatuma to the brink of death. Fatuma found herself embroiled in a difficult dilemma: whether to abandon her marriage and return to her parental abode, a pride price would have to be paid, namely the restitution of the cows that had been offered in exchange for her hand. Although the number of cattle had tripled over time, the weight of tradition lay not in their quantity, but in the very principle of the tradition itself. The cows that were once mere calves had proliferated into productive milch cows and sturdy plowing oxen, and Igwe and Mahanju had already expended most of them to satisfy their own bride prices. No one in the family was inclined to overturn this.

In these darkest hour, her husband remained indifferent to her plight, leaving her to suffer in silence. I was told she was left to concoct a "cure" from salt and traditional herbs, a futile effort to cure the unknown illness that afflicted her. Even in these extremes, such as when an individual's life was imperiled, her traditional parents found it more tolerable to endure the ignominy of their daughter's maltreatment in her marriage than to countenance her divorce. Her request to "come home" was to allow an egregious family dishonor, one that exceeded the scope of parental failure.

In our traditions, once a woman had been wedded, it is not deemed acceptable for her to return to her parents' domicile. Only a handful of parents had the fortitude to receive their "returning home" daughters from their husbands. Most parents were content to have their daughters remain for a short while when marital disputes arose. This meant that she could stay for a fortnight or less than a month as a means of mitigating her anger or reflecting on the abuse she had endured. After that period had elapsed, they would begin to show her the door: "go to your home," "you have your own house," "you have a husband," "everybody goes through this," "go to your children." That was Fatuma.

This was not the first instance of Fatuma returning home. According to my mother, every time she returned and complained of feeling unwell, her husband evinced no concern. She was never taken to any hospital. On the contrary, he would instruct her to mix salt, water, and some traditional herbs and drink it to allay the nausea. "Malaria does not require hospital-ization," she was told. But Fatuma was not suffering from malaria. No one even knew what was ailing her. She was never tested for malaria or anything else; even if she had been, she was simply left to languish. Despite her health deteriorating, she was a hapless woman.

The toll on her physical and emotional well-being was immeasurable, the pain and suffering etched deeply into her soul. During our meeting, I gazed upon the face of my sister, a mere shadow of the person I once knew. I was taken aback. This was not the Fatuma I knew, my "sister" and my uncle's daughter. Her level of exhaustion was unfathomable to me, and the trauma etched on her face was heart-wrenching. The way she looked at me, with eyes that seemed to convey that "nothing around me mattered anymore," was almost too much to bear. When she did manage to speak, it was through signs that conveyed the message that she didn't expect to live much longer. She was torn in every possible way, uncertain if staying at her mother's house would only bring more shame upon her or if leaving to be with her reckless husband would only lead to her demise.

Her husband was indifferent, never bothering to visit or inquire about her well-being. I couldn't believe that this was the same woman whom I had known to be so full of life, now reduced to being used and abandoned with no hope of a future. On my sight an example of casualty—a reminder of the pernicious consequences of patriarchal oppression and societal norms that silence the cries of the unheard. After all, wasn't it said that "women have no future; they live in the future of their husbands," or that if they did have a future, it remained undiscovered? Was it believed that a woman required a man to be deemed significant? In the case of my sister, she was nobody to anyone. She was trapped in a cycle of choiceless, a prisoner in her own home—the outcome of the system where a woman must attempt to survive a cruel fate that robbed her of her agency, her future, and her very life. Her husband's callous disregard for her health and welfare had left her with little hope, and in her despair, she felt she had no other option but to return to him.

My heart sank as I reflected on the day I left my home village of Mtinko a few days after meeting Fatuma in her parents' home. Although I had to return to complete my theological studies, thoughts of her consumed my mind. It was disturbing to witness how my own sister, a woman born to live a fulfilling and passionate life, had transformed into an emaciated and lackluster individual. How could a once-vibrant soul become a mere apparition of her former self? Even after my departure, I was told, she had tenaciously insisted, "I want to stay home, I am tired," but her plea fell on deaf ears. She was shown the door and ultimately coerced to return to her husband, as was expected of her. "We have all been through it. You must go back to your home," she was told. And so, Fatuma acquiesced. However, a few weeks later, news of her precarious health left her bed, and before her parents could get hold of the news, she was pronounced dead.

At the time of Fatuma's passing, I was still in Kiomboi. Although I had anticipated her demise after observing her condition a month earlier, the news still shook me to the core. The abrupt disappearance of a person is what makes death so unforgiving. Later, I asked my mother whether she knew what had killed Fatuma. She was unaware. As a newly "born again" Christian, she speculated, "Perhaps she was possessed by evil spirits." Until this day, the cause of her death remains a mystery. Whether her fate was preordained or not, Fatuma is no longer with us to speak for herself. She is at rest at last, and only the grave bears witness to her suffering.

Lost in thought about past memories, I nearly let them spoil my happiness in officiating Angela's wedding. These were memories that I often tried to suppress, but on this day, they stubbornly refused to be buried. I found myself pondering, "What is the true purpose of marriage? Why does society only show the positive aspects of marriage while ignoring the darker side?" As I gazed upon the faces of those in the church, they seemed to be wearing joyful smiles and singing with gusto, but I could sense their hearts were saying the opposite. "*Jambo usilolijua ni kama usiku wa kiza*"— something unknown is like a pitch-black night." This was what I thought married people felt deep down, but perhaps these were just my own delusions while standing at the pulpit.

I lifted my head and offered a rare smile. I could sense a tinge of fear and discomfort on the faces of the couple before me, but this too could have been a figment of my imagination. "Why do people choose to get married anyway?" I asked myself, my thoughts turning to Fatuma's untimely death. "What if Angela doesn't want to marry?" I debated within myself. "Why do I feel compelled to be part of this unnecessary tradition?" I questioned my role as a pastor as I reached for my Bible. The crowd was already paying close attention, eager to hear me preach. "What should I say? Love, endurance, or simply 'good luck'?"

****

"Why do you wish to be married?" I recall asking Angela a week before her wedding. Here was this lovely and guileless young lady who couldn't muster the courage to look me in the eyes. "Will you answer my question?" I pressed, hoping to gain more insight. "Yes, pastor," she replied, visibly uncomfortable, her gaze fixated on the ground. "I love him, pastor," she murmured, shyly concealing her smile. "Look at me, Angela. I am your spiritual guide, am I not?" I encouraged her, hoping to alleviate her anxiety. She lifted her head slightly, but quickly lowered it again.

This was during a premarital counseling session, where my role was to impart knowledge about wedding customs and marital life. I confess I felt inadequate, being unmarried myself and having no firsthand experience with marriage. The tragedy of Nikota's untimely death was still fresh in my mind, and it had instilled in me a certain sense of cynicism about love. I knew our men in Igengu did not place a great deal of value on love, but did Angela understand that they say "marriage is both paradise and hell?"

Time flew, and Angela's marriage ceremony was concluded. She and her new husband left Igengu happily to begin their new life in his village, which was located roughly twenty kilometers away. I left Igengu a year later and never heard from Angela again.

Several years later, while travelling on a public bus from Arusha to Singida, my hometown, a woman who had failed to pay her fare was being forcibly dragged out by a conductor. I could barely see her from my seat although unable to quite make out her features. At the Majengo area outside Arusha, the bus was forced to stop so that the woman could disembark. "My money is in my bag," she pleaded tearfully as the conductor roughly shoved her out the door. "I don't care! *Toka nje maza!* This isn't your father's bus! You think you're riding for free?" the conductor bellowed, devoid of any semblance of humanity. "I told you I'd pay you! Please wait, I can't reach my bag," she cried out, her efforts to resist the push proving futile.

As the drama unfolded, passengers in the bus began to voice their displeasure. "Why not listen to the lady, for heaven's sake!" they grumbled. The scene continued for several intense minutes until the bus finally came to a full stop. As the woman staggered between the bus door handle and the steps, she found herself on the edge of the road, and eventually collapsed on the pavement. Her khanga, which covered her waist, flew up and exposed her bare backside. As she composed herself, I realized that she was also pregnant.

In that moment, my soft yet resolute character took over. Whether due to her gravid state or the distressing situation, I felt compelled to confront the conductor. Rising from my seat, I shouted, "Hey! Take your money and let the woman on the bus!" My voice and rage seemed to fall on deaf ears as the conductor signaled for the bus to move. "Stop the bus, you fool, and let her in!" an angry passenger joined me.

Meanwhile, I struggled to make my way to the bus door where the conductor stood. At that moment, the woman on the ground collected herself and saw my face. "Pastor Kaghondi, help me, help me, please!" she cried out. "What did I hear?" I thought. "Did she just call me by my name?" It became clear to me that this stranger was someone I knew.

The situation was chaotic. The bus, which was supposed to have been in motion, remained stationary, even as it revved its engine impatiently. By now, I had reached the door where the woman was. I recognized the woman's voice, but I couldn't quite place her face. She attempted to gather her scattered belongings while holding onto the bus door with one hand. Suddenly, the bus began to move again. "Stop the bus, for heaven's sake!" we all screamed, brimming with fury. "Take her fare," I insisted. "This is what these people do. They flatter you until you pay up, and then they forget all about you. You care about money more than people!" An elderly woman behind me shouted indignantly at both the conductor and the driver. The bus screeched to a halt once more. "Can't you see that this woman is with child?" I demanded, my anger palpable. The conductor, meanwhile, seemed to have had a change of heart. "Hey, bro, it's not like that. This is a business, you know . . ." he began, attempting to justify his earlier actions. "Take her fare and let her board," I interjected, brandishing a ten-thousand-shilling note.

The bus came to a complete stop. The poor woman struggled to board. The conductor, shamed by the passengers, didn't even bother to collect the money from me. It wasn't until I took a closer look at her that I realized who she was: Angela, the same woman whose marriage I had officiated four years ago in Igengu. However, Angela looked nothing like the woman I remembered. Her facial appearance troubled me deeply. "What could have happened to her?" I wondered. I waited for her to take a seat on the bus and for things to settle down before I approached her. As passengers were dropped off along the way, the bus cleared up a bit, and I was able to sit next to her. When she confided in me about her situation, I was left aghast at the unspeakable horrors she had endured.

Angela had been physically abused by her husband since the day they were married. Despite several attempts to escape, she had been unable to do so until recently, when she convinced her husband that she needed to go home to visit her ailing mother. The mother was not really sick, of course. The plan was for Angela to use the opportunity to run away. However, her husband, suspecting what she might do, refused to let her go alone and decided to accompany her to Igengu.

The young couple had recently welcomed a child into the world. During their stay with Angela's parents, the couple was granted a separate dwelling on the homestead. Angela was finally safe and secure in her new-found refuge. Days turned into weeks, and she showed no inclination of returning to her husband's domain.

She was resolute in her decision to stay put, come what may. The husband, feeling cornered and powerless within the walls of his in-laws' *boma*, was unable to resort to his usual brutish tactics. He attempted to sway Angela to reconsider her stance, but she stood her ground and offered him three options: make a permanent home in Igengu, where she felt safe, return without her, or file for a divorce. While Angela felt empowered being in her parents' sanctuary, the man couldn't bear the argument and was left feeling emasculated. He needed to devise a plan, and fast.

Numerous nights were likely spent in restless contemplation. Eventually sleepless nights plagued the man as he tossed and turned, struggling to come to terms with his predicament. One night, while Angela was sound asleep, the man realized that reconciling with his wife was a futile endeavor. In a moment of desperation, he resolved not to lose alone.

Silently, he crept out of the house and into the darkness. As I previously mentioned, Igengu was a place of jagged rocks and rough terrain. When the man returned to the room, he approached Angela's bedside. Every member of the household was fast asleep, unaware of the impending tragedy. The devil had taken hold of him, and the man had transformed into a homicidal maniac.

He had collected a hefty rock, weighing approximately two kilos, from outside the homestead. As he stood beside Angela, he probably hoisted the rock into the air, swearing allegiance to the gods of murder. Whether he intended to kill or merely reclaim his masculinity, he hurled the rock down with every manly rage to land on the woman's delicate features. In a matter of seconds, a "sleeping beauty" was rendered unconscious.

Angela likely made nonsensical punches, floundering in a pool of her own blood. These incoherent movement and inhalations, coupled with a constricted throat, rapidly transformed the woman who was once a radiant angel into a denizen of the afterworld. Her husband, now a murderer, was fully cognizant of the gravity of his actions as he ran into the unknown. To underscore the enigmatic nature of Igengu, he vanished in the dark, never to be seen again.

No one in the household would have been privy to what occurred in the couple's quarters had it not been for the wailing of the infant. All members of the household were asleep, including Angela's parents. Perhaps due to the impact of the fatal blow or some divine intervention, the baby cried out pitifully, as if to announce that all was not well with her mother. "Why is the baby crying so inconsolably? Where are her parents?" Angela's mother would recount this tragic event the following morning.

The Swahili have a saying: *"Kama hujui kufa, tazama kaburi"*—If you do not know how to die, visit the graveyard. That was what it was for Angela's mother. She had been waked from sleep by the crying baby. If not for the baby, she would not have known anything from another side of the homestead. A sense of unease took hold of her as she ambled towards the hut where Angela, her spouse, and their infant slept. She tried calling out to Angela through the window but to no avail. A chill went down her spine as she listened intently to the crying of the baby. She knew that something was amiss.

She called after Angela through their window but received no response. As she tried to understand what kind of sleep these "lovers" slept to not hear their daughter, she realized that something unusual might have happened. She decided to break in, which parents would not traditionally do under normal circumstances. Surprisingly, the door was not even locked. Using dim firewood as a spotlight, the elderly mother walked in the room to be welcomed by nothing but the flood of blood on the very doorsteps.

The baby had wept almost to the point of losing her voice. Her mother, unclothed, lay lifeless, floating in a pool of suffocating blood. Angela's mother cried shockingly, the cry that woke up the neighbors. She rushed back to her hut to grab a bucket of cold water and powered on the assumably dead daughter. As if to confirm that miracles exist, that cold water brought Angela back to life. "She is still breathing," the villagers would recall reacting. With the help of neighbors, they brought her outside for fresh air. Her whole head was too soaked in blood for anyone to identify what had happened. The husband, not being there, was obviously the first suspect. Angela opened her eyes some hours later, and even when she was fully awake, she would never reconstruct any part of her own death. It was her mother that pieced it all together, speculating from the presence of the rock by the bed and the unlocked door.

Igengu is devoid of any hospitals, as previously mentioned. The only "dispensary" that existed was merely a futile promise from the MP during the last election, as its walls has never progressed beyond the foundation. As a result, Angela had to be transported on an oxcart for several kilometers to reach a place where she could catch a car to a hospital in a different district. Her injuries were severe, and she had lost all of her front teeth and suffered from fractured jaws, which explained the scars and disfigured face I saw when I met her on the bus.

Observing her appearance, I couldn't help but feel repulsed by the heinous act of cruelty that had transformed this woman into an unrecognizable being. Prior to this, I had never imagined such evil in the world, and it led me to question the very characters of my fellow African men.

Nevertheless, Angela survived against all odds, and while I believe God played a role in her recovery, I couldn't help but wonder why such a terrible incident would happen to someone who was so godly. Does God not know our future, or is this merely a part of his plan?

Despite surviving the attack, Angela's physical and emotional scars were deep, and the trauma of the attack had shattered her sense of self. She struggled to reconcile the person she was before with the person she had become after the attack. Her identity, once robust and self-assured, was now in a state of flux. She contemplated suicide. But somehow, she found the strength to keep going while wrestling with the reality of her place in society as a woman who had suffered such trauma. "Look at me!" she exclaimed, tears streaming down her disfigured face. "Do you think this is who I am?" Her once striking beauty was now a distant memory, replaced by toothless jaws and numerous stitches.

She chose to leave Igengu, vowing to disappear from this planet. I learned that she eventually had landed in Arusha. There, she found work as a housekeeper in the city. However, as unlucky as she was, she ended up being impregnated by who-knows-who in the city. Looking at her and trying to reconcile my memories of her wedding—if not for the sake of human desire, why would anyone get married?

IV

-

"When two bulls fight, the grass is what suffers"

—Swahili proverb

—

DURING MY TENURE AT Igengu, my friend Zahoro and I decided to cultivate a garden. We planted various greens such as spinach, Chinese cabbage, and okra. After a few months, our harvest surpassed our family's usage, despite being bachelors. Zahoro proposed the idea of selling the surplus vegetables to supplement my income, to which I agreed. We started trading a few stalks for a bowl of sorghum or corn, and eventually gathered enough to sell for profit. The sales were promising and covered most of our domestic needs.

Our garden was situated in a place called Mbugani, a low-lying, fertile soil region where locals grew sugar cane. Before reaching Mbugani was where Zahoro collected our drinking water, from a place that took me several months to locate, and when I finally did, I understood why the locals were hesitant to reveal it. Consequently, Zahoro was appointed to manage my daily chores, which included fetching water for the pastor and cooking.

Technically, the drinking water was drawn from the sandy riverbed. In the morning, women and girls from the village would venture down to the river to fetch water, often collecting from a running river during the rainy season. However, the river was seasonal, which means, in the dry season, it would only contain sand, and people had to dig out a few inches to wait for a few drops of water to collect in a small hole. After its sediment had settled at the bottom, the water was then scooped one bowl at a time to fill their thirsty buckets, while several patient hours were filled with gossip. The water was a brownish-dark liquid "thing" that tasted like urine when not boiled, and one could only wonder where it picked up its tantalizing aroma, as cows also shared the same river. In a place like this, what mattered most was the availability of water. Even when the bucket was heavier than it should be, it was less necessary to question whether water or amoeba filled it.

Zahoro was perhaps the luckiest one in the village, thanks to my pastoral bicycle. This Phoenix brand bike was a gift from American missionaries during my graduation from theological college, and it became a life-changer. First, the personal bicycle had become a public transportation medium. But more importantly, while the villagers could only carry one bucket at a time, Zahoro could transport up to four buckets at once. Sometimes, he would pile them up and try to carry as much as he could manage to get them across the sandy river. The pastor's bike had lost almost half its spokes, yet it was everything one could need in the village. As long as its wheels kept rotating and Zahoro didn't tumble into the ditch, we had drinking water.

These were a few of the moments that helped me feel grounded. The bicycle, garden, music, and church routines were my indeterminate schedule. I worked in the garden during the mornings and afternoons, and in the evenings, I spent most of my time at my house. Even if there was an empty muddy office, nothing was really scheduled for me. Only a few cases would emerge here and there during the week, but otherwise, the villagers did not need the pastor that much during the week. Sunday was the only day that everyone would bring their problems to the pastor.

Building connections was of paramount importance not just with Christians, but with everyone in the village. In a society that was community-based, connecting with people was not a daunting task as long as one engaged with the right ones. As I had previously mentioned, my house was in close proximity to a main path, and as expected of a pastor's home, all sorts of strangers would stop by as long as the door was ajar. Whenever the smoke from the charcoal stove dissipated, it almost signaled to the villagers that lunch was ready. If by any chance Zahoro and I found ourselves alone at the dining table, we considered that day a miracle.

From the doorstep, I had a bird's eye view of pedestrians strolling along the street. In the evening, my ears would be assailed by the off-key chanting of the inebriated strangers as they stumbled over the lyrics in an unpoetic fashion, tripping over rocks on the dusty street. Latecomers, including underage boys, would improvise tunes over pop songs on the local FM radio stations, their traditional singing accents squeaking alongside the boomboxes that were often slung over their shoulders by a shoelace. Over the course of months, I had absorbed every tune, every fart, every odor of urine, and every curse of beatings through my unsealed window. However, "time" has its own way of weaving magic, and eventually, my ears slowly became desensitized to such madness.

As I had mentioned earlier, my house was situated in this location by coincidence. It was located between the eastern and western parts of Igengu. The eastern side was known as Mbuyuni, and the western side was known as Madukani. These divisions served only some governing purposes; otherwise, Igengu was one village. They were what is known as "vitongoji." That way, each side had its local representative or official who was in charge of government directives.

Madukani means "shopping center," although only a handful of kiosks existed. Ideally, Madukani would be considered a "downtown" or "city center" if Igengu were a city. During the day, most young men gathered there to gossip if not at deer hunting. They would spend their entire afternoon pointing at girls' butts as they stopped at kiosks to buy kerosene or to mill corn flour in the nearby machine. Loudly, they would brag and argue about which girl each of them had "tested" and who the emerging prettiest woman in the village was. Gossip like this only stopped after one of their own sisters entered the scene. For that reason, if one were to alter a word, the whole scene would turn into a bloodbath. It was at Madukani side as well where the church building and the fallen-wall primary school were located.

Mbuyuni, on the other hand, was named after a large baobab tree. This was a famous ancient tree that had withstood the test of time. The tree was a meeting place for various rallies and gatherings in the village. When there were important matters that concerned the village, elders gathered under Mbuyuni to resolve them in a traditional manner.

Next to the baobab tree was a half-collapsed government office and the unfinished foundation of what was meant to be a two-room health center (dispensary). The dispensary was one of the campaign promises that perhaps needed another political campaign, that is, after five years, to have at least its wall raised. Anyhow!

Mbuyu and Madukani were linked by a pavement that traversed the house where I resided. Coincidentally, my home was situated equidistant between the two points, isolated from both ends. No other dwellings lay in proximity. If not for the continuous flow of passersby, this locale would have been a true paradise. Nonetheless, that was not the reality.

****

The allure of the full moon had beckoned me to seek out a rare breath of fresh air. Positioning my tripod stool beside the wall, I surrendered my self to a meditative version of utopia. Zahoro had departed to spend the night at his parents' abode. Igengu was quieter than usual, as if to provide a serene moment for me to digest the *ugali* and *nsansa* I had just consumed, while pondering what I should preach that Sunday. But tranquility is never long-lived in Igengu. Before I could fully settle into my thoughts, in the dim light of the moon, a woman, who would later be identified as Janet, hastily approached my doorstep. She had been running and only slowed down upon entering my yard. She walked past me, almost oblivious to my presence, to knock on the door. Seeing her from afar, I had already braced myself for the worst.

"What is it? What is it?" I inquired anxiously, suspecting that she had been beaten by her husband. "My husband . . ." She stumbled over her words as if unprepared to speak. "What?" She took a short breath, rubbed her face with the back of her palm, and tried to force the sentence out. "Tell me—what happened?"

"Did your husband beat you?" I hastily jumped to a conclusion, looking straight at her face to see if she had any signs of physical violence. "No! My—my husband is . . . he is being killed." "Being killed? By whom? What happened? Tell me what happened," I commanded, shaking her by both shoulders. She summoned the courage to explain.

One hundred or more men from Mbuyuni had gathered beneath the baobab tree, planning an attack against the Madukani men. They were the village warriors, carrying machetes, spears, knives, heavy clubs, and all the necessary weapons, with the mission to "catch" or "kill" Jacob. "I overheard them discussing killing my husband. They are on their way now, pastor. My husband is going to be killed—help me!" Janet cried on my shoulder.

"What? Oh my God! What is wrong with you people?" I panicked. "I was not prepared for this . . . what do you . . ." I stumbled over my words as if Janet was the reason. "I don't know, Pastor! They will kill him."

Some months before, after I arrived at Igengu, I was informed that Janet's marriage was on the rocks. The couple had appeared calm at the elders' council at the time of my arrival, but things had escalated in recent days, and I was unaware of it. As Janet and I spoke, she was partially divorced. I learned this fact on the spot. Therefore, Jacob had sent her back to her parents' house. Usually, being sent home like this means being divorced or put on probation. If on probation, this time is allocated for the wife to "learn how to live with her husband from her mother." This was a euphemism for "your mother didn't prepare you to be a wife." That's how it is: all the faults of female children are attributed to their mothers, while their accomplishments are linked to their fathers. Anyhow!

In some instances, a wife who is sent home would not know whether it meant a complete divorce or a partial one. Only time would tell if the husband would come back for a second chance or not. If he didn't, then it would be considered a total divorce. At least that was a cultural form of divorce, and other procedures would follow to return the dowry.

I was told that Janet and Jacob frequently quarreled because her husband had accused her of infidelity while he was away. For some reason.

Their troubles began after the birth of their last daughter, when Jacob refused to believe that the baby was his and instead accused Janet of bearing another man's child. In our culture, men sometimes assume the role of a deity. Their perception can be more accurate than DNA tests when it comes to identifying if the child resembles them. The rumors among people supported his suspicions. However, Janet had maintained that the child was his, but Jacob never believed her.

Since then, Janet had been living a miserable life, practically forcing herself to stay in the marriage. Because they were married in church, Jacob found it difficult to divorce her as he had no concrete evidence. But he chose to be impolite to her as a way of pushing her out of the marriage. Every time the woman took the matter to the church, they asked him about it, and he would either deny or argue, "If I am that rude, then why is she still with me?" And the woman wouldn't initiate the divorce because she knew it was a trap. The whole drama went back and forth, and no one wanted to initiate the divorce to avoid looking bad in the eyes of the church. According to the church rules, the one who initiates the divorce is viewed as the cause of the problems and is likely to be excommunicated for going against the Bible/faith. As a result, the victim is likely to be punished. That was Janet's dilemma amidst a turbulent marriage. But that was not why Janet came to my house that evening. What brought her here was the remnants of "love" or the proof that even when love has failed, "humanity" can still save us.

To put the story into context, Janet and Jacob's apartment was located on the Madukani side, although Janet was born on the Mbuyuni side. Miraculously, her parents' house was a few feet away from the baobab tree where the meeting was being held. On this day, while the Mbuyuni warriors were planning to invade Madukani and "capture" or "kill" Jacob (Janet's husband), Janet and her mother happened to be listening from their house. The crowd did not know that Janet was home, except for her father, who was present at the meeting but could not go against the elders. The warriors were directed to first capture Jacob, who was the leader of the Madukani gang, and kill him if necessary.

Earlier, I had mentioned that Janet was on a sort of "marriage probation." However, upon hearing the plan to kill the man with whom they shared so much, her feminine instincts kicked in, and she simply couldn't sit idly by. Setting aside their differences, and considering the well-being of her children, she snuck out of the house and ran to warn Jacob of the impending danger. This was a risky move, as being caught by the elders would have dire consequences. At that time, Jacob was completely oblivious to the fact that his life was in danger. Had he been a prophet, he would have foreseen that "today, people needed his head."

While en route to warn Jacob, Janet had a change of heart and decided to speak with me first, fearing that her husband would not believe her. That was the reason for her visit to my house.

"Janet, I cannot let this happen. You must speak with your husband and urge him to leave," I advised.

"No, Pastor! My husband divorced me. He won't listen to me. If he sees me, he will kill me," she responded, her voice shaking with fear.

"You are not divorced, Janet. Go to him and tell him that I sent you. He will listen to me. Let me know if he ignores you. Does he want to die?" I insisted, my words somewhat incoherent, yet convinced that Jacob would heed my warning.

"Okay, Pastor. I will go," Janet reluctantly agreed, and then she disappeared into the darkness.

"Make sure to come back to me. Do you hear me?" I whispered to myself, doubting my decision to send Janet in my place. "If he refuses, tell him I sent you, and then you. . ." I continued giving instructions, although Janet was already out of sight. A long silence followed.

Since I had arrived in Igengu, Jacob had shown me great respect. Although he was a member of my church, his marriage had caused him to backslide. I had first met him at Mbugani, where he had a large sugarcane field near our garden. Every morning, Zahoro and I would go to water our garden, and Jacob would be there, always offering us sugarcane. However, his kindness did not guarantee that he was a decent man. I knew that he had a darker side, which made him unpopular in the village. However, this evening, I was confident that Jacob would not ignore Janet's warning, relayed through me.

As I watched Janet run off to save her husband, I felt a wave of nausea engulf me. "I have sent a woman to her death. This could end in tragedy," I thought to myself. "I should have gone myself." My worries only intensified when I realized that Janet could be caught by the Mbuyuni men and beaten to death for being a traitor. "I will never forgive myself for this mistake," I muttered to myself.

As I sat there in the darkness, waiting for Janet to return with no success. The safety of a woman was at stake, and I felt the weight of that responsibility on my shoulders. Despite my initial confidence in Jacob's willingness to heed my warning, doubt crept in as the minutes turned into hours. I tried to push those thoughts aside and focus on the belief as small as a mustard seed.

Now I must revisit the origin of this tragedy. Prior to Janet's visit to my home a few days earlier, there was a soccer tournament between the Madukani and Mbuyuni teams, which I previously mentioned. The teams were vying for the "MP's cup." As I stated before, politicians are considered "the people's men" but only during campaign seasons. In this instance, a political candidate who was campaigning for a seat in parliament had provided a soccer ball and a dozen jerseys to attract villagers. These items bore his name and party to advertise his involvement in "community work." While these may seem like mere trinkets, to the villagers, they were valuable enough to sway their opinions. What others refer to as "bribery," we call "gratuity" in our country. This is how corrupt politicians have maintained their grip on power for so long.

The gifts were insufficient for every team, thus they had to be competed for and distributed to the winning team. That team would then be named the "MP's cup champion." The tournament began with youth teams playing in groups. These teams were mostly comprised of young men who had never had an opportunity to play with a real soccer ball, let alone wear professional jerseys or shoes. The most desperate part of a man in the village, after his penis, is probably his bare feet for a soccer ball.

I attended the final match, which was between the Mbuyuni and Madukani teams. As the game progressed towards the ninetieth minute, the two teams were nearly equal. A few minutes before the game ended, a voice (presumably that of a drunken man) was heard from the crowd, cursing a referee for favoring the Madukani team. While spitting out his verbal abuse disrespectfully, the man swayed across the line that separated the fun from the players. Suddenly, the cheering crowd from Madukani began to insult him. Some were unable to resist approaching him. In no time, he had been dragged aside and his shirt was torn badly.

As this was happening, the Mbuyuni cheering group came to defend him. Before we knew it, the madness had spread throughout the field. People from the other end began crossing over the field to join in the ongoing chaos, while some were already hurling rocks at both teams. Players in the field were also throwing punches at each other and arguing over unfair play. The game had stopped to give violence time to achieve its objective.

Violence is like a bull waiting for a poke. In a fragile railing like Igengu, violence requires no justification to erupt. And when two bulls fight, the grass is what suffers. The game had poked the Igengu bulls, and the village was consumed by madness. What had been a soccer field had turned into a war zone. Fire, rocks, and sticks were all flying through the air. The fortunate ones were those at home, at least for the moment.

The entire field was a swarm of people at that moment. Individuals from the surrounding area came to observe or be a part of the chaos. Players in the field had been fighting among each other, while others chased the referee who was already running off the field to save his life. I grabbed my old bicycle and ran for my life. I would never find out what happened next in the midst of the chaos and uproar that night. Of course, anyone with a clear mind would not be able to explain exactly what was going on.

I later learned that the drunk man miraculously survived, though that was not the end of the saga. Thank God nobody was killed, but unfortunately, many were injured, and much property was destroyed. Of course, the game ended without a winner.

The Madukani team accused the Mbuyuni team of "using" the drunk man to ruin the match, while the Mbuyuni team also accused Madukani of "bribing" the referee. Then, Madukani, the host of the game, decided to declare themselves as the winners. They marched towards the award ceremony, determined to claim the trophy by force. They collected the award, which was a box of soccer jerseys and a soccer ball donated by the MP candidate.

The situation was so vicious that the game "officials" who were still holding the box could no longer hold on to it. They had to run and hide, leaving the items behind. After the Madukani team seized the trophy, they began chanting and singing as they walked downtown, completely disregarding the chaos they had caused. Meanwhile, the Mbuyuni team and their supporters had retreated to their homes, located to the east, past my house.

Things were supposed to be over then, but not in Igengu, where conflicts are not won but lost. I went to bed that evening thinking, "Fine, let's say the Madukani team won," but I underestimated what the Mbuyuni men were capable of. Retaliation is a way of life in Igengu, something that I had almost forgotten about.

The following morning, I went to water my garden and found out that a mob from Mbuyuni had sneaked out during the night and set fire to the Madukani sugar plantations. Some of these plantations belonged to Madukani individuals who were accused of playing unfairly and forcibly declaring themselves as winners. As expected, only Mbuyuni people were accused of such destruction. Thus, the saga began.

Over the following week, revenge skirmishes went back and forth, with villagers' farms, gardens, and properties from both sides being completely destroyed. Among the farms that were severely burned belonged to Jacob, Janet's husband. He was suspected of being the leader of the mob that set fire to Mbuyuni's farms. Jacob was the type of person who seemed favorable to such actions, having been associated with other problems in the community before. It seemed to me that the Mbuyuni men had wanted him dead even before this incident happened. Now that it had, they had a good reason to kill him. But as others would say, "miracles exist." Janet, his wife, happened to get hold of the baobab tree plan and destroyed the entire scheme. However, she was nowhere to be found to give me the feedback.

Let's return to the night when Janet visited me. The distance between my house and Jacob's house was less than a fifteen-minute walk, so Janet shouldn't have been gone for long. However, she did not return, and my heart began to pound heavily in my chest. I couldn't bring myself to go to sleep, and the uncertainty was overwhelming. I considered following her but ultimately decided against it.

Suddenly, out of nowhere, a mob of at least seventy men carrying local weapons emerged from the darkness. These, as Janet had warned me, were the Mbuyuni warriors. I was completely unsure how to respond and found myself walking closer to the street. I knew that most people in the village knew me and that they would not harm me. Despite the dim light, I could recognize many faces in the mob, including Musa, Hassan, and Yohana, among others. Some of them even attended the church where I served as a pastor. They continued to march forward with their spears and clubs, like Roman soldiers carrying out the emperor's orders to detain a Jew.

Musa quietly approached me. He was carrying a machete in his right hand and a club in his left. I was shocked to see him there and whispered his name in a commanding tone, asking him what was going on. "Musa, what are you doing?" I demanded an explanation. "This was my church member," I thought to myself. "How could a church member be planning to kill someone?"

"Pastor! We have been given orders by the elders to bring Jacob to justice," Musa said, his voice trembling with fear.

"Justice? What kind of justice?" I demanded, my heart racing with anxiety and confusion. "And who is Jacob? Is he a criminal mastermind with an army of his own?" I asked, incredulous at the sight of so many men armed with weapons.

"Well . . . he's a troublemaker," Musa stuttered, struggling to explain the situation.

"A troublemaker? And you need all of these men to apprehend him? Do you honestly believe he's capable of taking on this many people, let alone own a machine gun?" I asked, my frustration growing with each passing moment.

But Musa didn't seem convinced. "Pastor, we are afraid. Jacob is a strong man," he replied, his voice barely above a whisper.

"This is madness!" I exclaimed. "Musa, please, think about what you're doing. You're a Christian, for God's sake!" I implored him, hoping to reason with him.

But Musa seemed to have made up his mind. "I'm sorry, Pastor. We have to follow the orders. And there are more men coming from all directions," he said, pointing towards the riverbed and the other end of the road. "We have to catch Jacob."

I felt a wave of panic wash over me. "This is worse than I thought," I said, feeling helpless and desperate. "What has this community come to? How can you all blindly follow these orders without question?" I yelled at him, my anger rising uncontrollably. But it was too late. Musa had joined the rest of the mob, disappearing into the darkness with their weapons raised high. And I was left alone, standing in shock and disbelief, wondering what had become of my community and the people I thought I knew.

As I stood there, watching the group of men disappear into the darkness, my heart was heavy with disappointment and disbelief. How could these church members abandon their Christian principles and blindly follow the elders' directives? The concept of justice had been warped and distorted by the traditions of the community, and it was disheartening to witness the extent of their loyalty to these archaic customs.

As the moon began to set and darkness crept in, Musa and several other men expressed their concern about going against the elders' orders. The penalty for disobedience could be hefty, ranging from a fine of several cows to complete excommunication from community. In a community like Igengu, membership in the group was paramount, with mere existence coming second. To belong to the community meant to abide by its rules or face the prospect of a nearly unbearable life.

Caught in a dilemma between tradition and Christianity, Musa seemed embarrassed by his own words, but he still chose to walk away. He promised he wouldn't harm anyone and would fight from behind. He assured me that he wasn't alone from the church and that Musa, Yohana, Matulu, and many others were also part of the group. "We have to pretend to be a part of it, even if we don't want to," Musa whispered.

"But Musa, I cannot condone this evil. What if you end up getting killed? I am not prepared to conduct your burial, Musa. This is devilish . . . stop!" I said in a fury, as if my words could make a difference. Musa left anyway.

As the night grew darker, I couldn't shake off the feeling of unease that had settled within me. Musa's words echoed in my mind, and I couldn't help but think of the dangers that lay ahead for him and the others. I couldn't comprehend why they would put themselves in harm's way, all for the sake of preserving a tradition that had lost its relevance.

My frustration boiled over, and I yelled out into the night, hoping that my voice would reach them. "Is this what it means to be a Christian in Igengu? To blindly follow orders and put your life at risk for the sake of tradition?" My words hung in the air, unanswered.

That's when I learned the hard way that there was little I could do except pray in silence. In less than an hour, the peaceful evening in the village had transformed into a scene of war. People who had been calm earlier in the day were now heading out to kill. It was disheartening to learn that some of the people involved in the violence were members of my own congregation. And yet, there was no sign of Janet's return, and I couldn't be sure what her disappearance meant. With my own church members involved in the plan to "catch" or "kill" Jacob, what else could I expect?

As I wandered outside my house, consumed with stress and anxiety, a sudden cry came from the direction of Madukani. I froze, trying to make sense of it, and a moment later I heard a few people running haphazardly past my house. They sounded frightened and disoriented. At that point, I decided to retreat to the safety of my home and leave everything to fate. I didn't hear anything more until I finally managed to fall asleep after a nightmarish ordeal.

When I woke up the next morning, I expected to see the village soaked in blood. But things were different. As it turned out, Jacob had been warned by Janet and had fled his house. However, he was too smart for his enemies. He went out to organize his men to defend themselves, choosing only a select few. They went to the Madukani area and hid among the fields. So when the Mbuyuni people surrounded Jacob's house, hoping to catch him off guard, he was not there. They did not realize that his house was empty, except for his cows in the kraal.

So they began to narrow their search, throwing spears randomly towards the cattle's kraal and shouting, "Come out, come out. Today is your day, Jacob!" Unbeknownst to them, Jacob's gang was behind them, and they were about to fall into a regrettable ambush. None of them could have predicted this surprise attack. It would prove that in a war, it is not just the fighters but also their strategies that determine the outcome.

Petrified and unprepared, the Mbuyuni warriors, though numerous, found themselves drinking from the cup of their own viciousness. Three of their men were captured by Jacob and his men. Initially, the thought of slaughtering the captives crossed their minds, but they ultimately decided to spare their lives out of a sense of humanity. One of the captives lost his fingers, another received a deep cut on his forehead from a panga, and the third was beaten so badly on his knees that he could no longer walk.

The rest of the Mbuyuni group scattered like unattended sheep, and in the morning, the elders agreed that the captives must be released. However, they had to pay for the collateral damage caused, including the cows that were speared to death at Jacob's home and a fine. The elders from both sides sat down to conduct reconciliatory meetings, and traditional methods were used to resolve the issue. Soon, Igengu returned to normal as if nothing had happened.

Regarding Jacob and Janet, I hoped that this incident would change Jacob's relationship with his wife. In my opinion, a woman like Janet, who sacrificed her life to serve her husband, was worth keeping. However, as is often the case in many Tanzanian cultures, men find it difficult to surrender their manly egos, and Jacob was no exception. He officially divorced Janet before I left Igengu, and he never returned to the church.

V

-

"Speak the truth or swallow a rock?"

—Arimi wisdom

—

To THEIR WIVES, MEN only let go of their secrets as a means of apology. Otherwise, they may not do so if they had not been caught in the act. On the other hand, women are seen as unforgiving creatures and thus may share theirs to face the consequences. This may be why African women have learned to listen more than speak up, out of fear of retribution. Conversely, men are not afraid to speak, but they may be afraid to listen.

It is not that women do not speak, but they often communicate more thoughtfully, with their souls instead of their mouths, especially when it comes to relationships. When a woman speaks her soul, she may divulge everything that has been weighing on her, as women tend to harbor emotions and feelings for long periods. They may pour out their hearts, knowing that they are ready to face the consequences. In contrast, a man's heart may only speak fragments of the truth, as it may be solely focused on self-defense. After spending a year in Igengu, I arrived at the conclusion.

The veracity of rumors was more powerful than that of truth in our culture. Whether or not Janet engaged in infidelity is not the main topic of our discussion. Even if she had engaged in such an act, would she have been able to accept it? "Truth is a dangerous thing," an elder once told me. "There are some things that must be swallowed," he insisted. The elder, a retired pastor, seemed to speak to me as if to challenge the biblical verse that states "the truth will set you free." He did not interpret those words the way I did. "These words are not to be taken literally, young man," he emphasized. As he continued his lecture to a young pastor, he explained how "truth" and "secrets" were nearly two sides of the same coin. Both of them contained the potential to ignite a fire that could consume an entire village if not handled with care.

Throughout his years in ministry, the retired pastor had witnessed the sweeping tide of Pentecostalism engulfing mainstream churches in Africa. The fervor of the Holy Ghost, especially in Tanzania, ignited new believers who flocked to public rallies hosted by American televangelists. The focus was on cleansing themselves of their old ways, carrying the "cross" of total repentance, and rejecting their parents and relatives to join the "heavenly membership." "Being born again" became a song on their lips as they spoke in tongues, slept in church, prayed aloud, and gave testimonies. They surrendered their entire lives to Jesus, crucifying what was referred to as "the ancient Adam." "The hour of salvation is now, the day of judgment is now, Jesus is coming now!" the preacher proclaimed into the microphone.

Whether by emphasizing the power of truth or by underestimating the devil's invisibility, people began to pour onto the stage. On their knees, they crawled with tears of confession to the preacher. "What happened in the dark must be brought to light," the preacher said. "Put the devil to shame," they were told. People gained the courage to be set "free." "The truth will set you free," the man of God proclaimed. "Bring the microphone—to put the devil to shame." Mega speakers were cranked up to the maximum volume—to broadcast people's confessions of their secrets. One by one, they lined up: "Before I gave my life to Jesus, I was a witch . . . before I repented, I was greedy . . . thank God I am born again!" The crowd cheered, "Hallelujah! Thank you, Jesus!" But before the community knew it, what had started as "good news" was not good at all.

The story of Mpandi and his wife is a testament to this craziness. The couple had raised four grown children and had lived peacefully throughout their marriage, until the day the "truth" sought to burst forth from the wife's soul. The two had come a long way as a couple. The man had found his wife in the remote regions of the country, uneducated and unemployed. With the meager earnings he made as a school cook, Mpandi had put his wife through nursing school. After graduating with her nursing diploma, she secured a job in a regional hospital. "They had finally escaped the hardships of the third world," people said.

They had been blessed with four children. As they entered the situation I am about to explain, their firstborn son had become a professional teacher, the second a self-made businessman, the third was in his final year of college, and the last one, their only daughter, had just completed her secondary education and was ready for college. If there was one thing the family could be proud of, it was their investment in their children's future through education.

Throughout their marriage, Mpandi was unaware of a crucial fact—he was not the biological father of his four children. This knowledge would later become a burden for everyone involved. As the Swahili proverb goes, "The bite of bedbugs is known only to a bed sleeper." Only Mrs. Mpandi knew the truth about what had happened in their marriage, and she understood the circumstances better than anyone else. However, others were unable to make sense of what had occurred.

From the outside, the Mpandis' marriage appeared to be perfect. The couple had managed to keep their secrets hidden until almost retirement age. But suddenly, either due to a desire to be free or a need to relieve herself of the burden of lies, Mrs. Mpandi chose to reveal her long-held secret to her husband. "These are not your children," she told him, insisting on the truth despite the potential consequences.

Whether due to the power of the "truth," which was now backed up by her newfound born-again faith, or a need to be set free, she began to reveal the true identity of each child's biological father. Her firstborn was revealed to be the offspring of a hospital director in the nearby region, who was perhaps unprepared to explain the situation to his own wife if that was his typical method of tending to his patients. The second child belonged to a well-known politician who may not have considered the ramifications of his public office. Her third child was revealed to be the child of a businessman, who now had to gamble to save his marriage. Finally, her last born was assigned to a college professor who had to explain to his family how his doctorate had ended up in another man's wife.

The marriage, which had once been a model of a church-going couple, was shattered into pieces. And Mpandi was left to choose between upholding his Christian faith or cursing the very religion that had destroyed his marriage.

The truth was a bitter pill to swallow. It broke Mpandi's heart and tore the children apart. The entire village was shaken by the revelation. In a small community where the sense of security depended on the "bond," people asked, "Was this truth necessary?" "Why didn't she just keep the secret if she had lived with it for all these years?" But as others said, "The bite of bedbugs is known only to a bed sleeper."

Some blamed Mpandi for the situation. "He should not have educated a woman," they said. Others ridiculed him for fertility issues—"he could not start his fire." For Mrs. Mpandi, who was a new convert to Christianity, the truth had set her free.

This all occurred before I became a pastor. I have since debated the morality of truth in marriage with myself. Perhaps what keeps marriages alive is not "love" or "truth" but "secrets." If Mrs. Mpandi had kept her secrets to herself, would her husband have known the difference? Now that the truth has been exposed, everyone involved is being punished—the families of the men with whom she had affairs, their wives, and the children who have grown up to learn about their half-siblings through another woman. How do grown-up children make sense of their parents' infidelity?

As a pastor, I have wondered what I would have advised Mrs. Mpandi if she had come to me for guidance about whether or not to confess about her infidelity. For now, I will leave this question unanswered for readers to ponder.

****

As I lay in my bed, still in the hazy grip of sleep, a gentle knock sounded at my door. A woman stood outside, her eyes downcast and her demeanor hesitant. "I need to talk to you," she said quietly, and I invited her in.

Her name was Jonita. Jonita was a married woman who was actively involved in the church, along with her husband and their two children. Her husband was a dedicated member of the congregation who often traveled to buy fish from a wholesale market across the region to trade for money or corn. Despite my initial impression of their marriage being a content one, Jonita's visit had me questioning what lay beneath the surface.

The couple had been my acquaintances since my arrival in Igengu, and they never missed a Sunday service. They were soft-hearted, and on their way home from church, they often stopped by my house to ensure that "our pastor had what he needs." They lived on the Mbuyuni side of the village, and I had visited their home several times. Based on my observations, their family seemed to be as good as it could be in such a dusty village.

But as Jonita began to speak, I realized that there was much more to her story. She confessed that she had been unable to sleep, that she could no longer bear the weight of her secret. "I'm tired of this," she said, her voice strained. "I cannot do this anymore." I was puzzled, unsure of what she meant. "Tired of what?" I asked, hoping to gain some clarity.

However, when Jonita spoke of being "tired," she also mentioned that she wanted to reveal "the truth." The word "truth" made me anxious, as I recalled what happened to Mpandi years ago. "What is it?" I asked, trying to calm myself. This was one of those days when you don't really want to know, but at the same time, you feel compelled to find out. "I am listening," I reassured her.

Jonita took a deep breath, indicating that what she was about to say might be unbearable. Although her arrival was less dramatic than Janet's, the suspense was still killing me. "I will just say it—the way it is. I want to say it," she struggled. "Take your time," I reassured her. After a long pause, she finally found the courage to confess, "I'm having an affair—with Samson."

"Samson?"

"Yes," I replied.

"But he—Samson is married . . ." I found myself giving a superfluous remark.

Samson was one of the most esteemed individuals in the congregation. He was one of the pillars of the church and had served in different capacities of leadership. It was due to the trust that Jonita had in him that she approached him for marital advice. However, instead of providing spiritual guidance, Samson offered a practical solution to Jonita's marital issues.

"He became close to me . . ." Jonita said, her voice trailing off. "I wanted him to help me enjoy my husband, because, really, I don't enjoy my marriage," she explained, her eyes welling up with tears. "As a man of God, I believed he would be able to help my marriage . . ." she added, her voice choked with emotion.

I learned that their so-called "counseling sessions" progressed into intimacy, and their story followed the familiar path. As these kinds of stories go, they counted on the "devil" for their human desires, while trading their spirituality with allure. The victim and exploiter seduced each other. That was what Jonita disclosed.

What began with prayer gradually shifted to caressing. And before reaching "amen," things had advanced to fondness. "We didn't know what we were doing," she offered in her defense, which was something I disagreed about. "We did only once, but we let ourselves do it again," as if they were not aware of what the Swahili saying warns: "*Muonja asali haonji mara moja*"—a honey taster never scoops once. Yet, Jonita insisted, "it was Samson's idea; it was his fault. As a man of God, he should have known better. He knew what we were doing was wrong!" she once again offered in her defense. At this time, I am listening for her to say it all. "He knows the Bible more than me, and. . ." She went on and on with that "blah blah" to honey-coat her side of the story.

Some say that the human soul is impossible to fulfill, while others say that the human heart is an ocean to cover. The search for fulfillment among the two went on unnoticed, until that week when Jonita woke up from her love fantasy to realize that "every penis is a penis." The affair had led a "counselor" and a "counselee" nowhere, except to register in their brains that they were Christians and married.

But by this point, the affair had gone deeper, causing them both to turn a blind eye. As people say, "love is blind," and Jonita was afraid that her husband was about to find out soon. "I decided that it is better that I tell you first before he finds out," she confessed. "I know that if my husband finds out from you, he will not be too angry. I want to save my marriage," she hoped. "I still love my husband," she said, though I wasn't sure if I believed it. And so, that was the reason that Jonita came to me. She wanted to ask me to talk to her husband—assuring him that she was guilty and ready to confess her sins and repent.

The biblical formula for repentance is forgiveness, but I often wonder how does a mere phrase like "I'm sorry" suffice for such a complex case? Where should one begin to tackle a case that involved not just lust but also lives, families, and the entire church community in a fragile congregation such as Igengu? Shouldn't Christians lead by example? I could almost hear non-believers snickering and see some members leaving the church. The story of Mpandi, which had haunted me before, returned to my mind.

What would the revelation do to their marriage, families, and the public? Would it not shatter the congregation and send people back to their old ways? If Samson, who was at the forefront of serving lost souls in Igengu, and Jonita, whose presence in worship was essential to Sundays, could do such things, what was the point of people coming to church? When the truth is as complex as a rock in the middle of a last chew, should it be spat or swallowed? I debated as Jonita poured her heart out to me on a Saturday morning. Should I disclose the truth or cover it up?

"We need to talk," I told Msengi after the worship. In case rumors began to circulate, I knew I had to act quickly, as Msengi had just returned from his business trip the night before. So, after the worship, I cautiously broached the topic in their living room, requesting Samson to join me without revealing the matter at hand. "What is this about this couple, pastor?" Samson had inquired on our way to the house, visibly concerned. "I'll explain when we get there," I responded, trying to conceal my anger. From that moment on, I attempted to steer clear of any further discussions.

In the house, Jonita was already weeping against the wall. Her husband, still in a daze, uttered, "You surprised me pastor—is everything okay?" I could not respond properly, but simply said, "I hope so," while taking a seat. The four of us were present for this conversation, but only Jonita and I knew the reason why we were there. Neither Samson nor Msengi knew what was coming. I mustered up some courage and began the conversation: "My dear friend Msengi," in a gentle tone, "this will not be easy for you to hear, but I implore you to listen to me and to handle it in a Christian manner." I prepared him vaguely. What followed was the "truth" that no man would ever want to hear about his wife. The truth that no pastor would want to deliver to his congregants.

A cheated man is a lion. How do you calm down a man who has just found out that his wife cheated on him? After explaining the situation, both Msengi and Samson were left speechless. I then began the arduous task of reconciling Msengi with his wife. I cannot recall how many hours it took to calm him down. Next, I moved on to reconciling Msengi with Samson. At this point, Msengi was grinding his teeth, pointing his finger at Samson in every furious manner possible: "Samson, if this pastor were not here, I would have chopped off your head." Samson had no words to utter. He had surrendered his entire manliness to the living room. "I have nothing to say, Bwana Msengi. I am truly sorry. I know you have every right to kill me."

A caught man was cold and powerless, like a chick in the rain. His penis was frozen like that of a cowardly dog. I was fuming with fury, unable to avert my gaze from him. Then the matter moved between Samson and Jonita. "What should I do to you?" I asked them with a human anger on my face. Hours of emotional exhaustion had passed. This emotional torture would finally lead to something tangible—Msengi had agreed to forgive his wife and Samson. At least that was what came from his mouth.

I have to mention that I had to treat this case as a matter of serious secrecy. There was so much at stake in exposing Samson and Jonita to the church public. Any leaking news, I believed, would have collapsed the entire church. The two were pillars of the church in many ways. For better or for worse, I chose to keep it between ourselves, and I kept Samson's wife out of it.

This may have played into my manly bias or cultural privilege. To this day, I am not sure whether hiding the matter from Samson's wife was just. Again, that begs the question: speaking the truth or swallowing the rock? Was it necessary to let a happy wife know that her husband had an affair? Or was it better to keep her out of the equation and save her from being hurt? That, I have to say, was a miserable day.

Ultimately, I believe that Samson and Jonita were genuinely forgiven by both the man and God. What else should a pastor do after repentance? However, as respected members of the church, they had lost their status. "You are forgiven, but you can no longer serve in any church role," I told them the following day. "I understand," Samson replied softly with gratitude. I stripped them of all their positions, and from that day, nobody would ever understand why they would never lead church programs again.

Nevertheless, the church community murmured, and curiosity grew. "What did Samson do?" people asked. "Why isn't Jonita leading XYZ?" the congregation wondered. I sealed my mouth, recalling the wisdom of my elders: "*mira nkomango*"—swallow the rock. "Pastoral duties," I would reply to their speculations.

Jonita's relationship with her husband became more strained afterwards. It was clear that Msengi had never recovered from his wife's infidelity. Recalling the story of Mpandi, I wondered whether this would have been the case if Jonita had not disclosed her secret to her husband. If Msengi had not known, perhaps it would not have damaged their marriage. Is that not a reward of ignorance? However, Jonita would have remained a slave to her deception. Now that Msengi knew the truth, he could not go back to the way things were. He divorced her.

For Samson's wife, the situation was different. She was kept in the dark, and their marriage survived. More than seven years later, Samson reached out to me on the phone. Among other things, he still recalled that disgrace and expressed his sincere gratitude for how I handled it. He and his wife were still "happily" married. He said he had "learned his lesson" and "truly regretted" his actions. At least that's what he told me. But I still wonder if I should have chosen truth over peace. I chose peace and jeopardized truth. Should the light of truth be revealed to those who are culturally blind? That is for the reader to judge.

When I bring these cases together—the case of Msengi and his wife, Janet and Jacob, Samson and Jonita, and Mpinda and his wife—I often wonder when truth helps or destroys. When do secrets rescue or ruin relationships? For now, I will leave this judgment to the reader.

VI

-

"A man's poo is inodorous"

—Arimi proverb

—

"A MAN'S POO IS inodorous," my mother once told me sarcastically, meaning men do not do mistakes. In Swahili, there is another similar saying that states "*mkubwa hajambi*," meaning seniors never fart, which is not to be taken literally. Even if Samson's wife had known of her husband's affair, I believe she would have forgiven him. In our cultures, the sin of a man is considered a mistake while that of a woman is a disgrace.

I was old enough to remember, but not mature enough to decipher, my mother's riddle. During story time on our patio, my father shared a tale of a dispute between an imaginary man and his wife while we waited for dinner. My dad was a representative in the village council, also known as *mjumbe wa nyumba kumi*, which entailed administrative and counseling responsibilities. He communicated top governmental messages to local citizens, addressed their concerns to the council, and settled community conflicts. This story seemed to draw from his experience in the council.

The story my father shared was in the form of a legend and involved a man named Makuja and his wife Nyamalwe, but I couldn't discern if the characters were real. Makuja had left the village to fish across the big ridge, a common practice for men who sought work after harvesting season. Some went to *Muria* for salt mining, others to *Magugu* to raise onions,

58

Sukumaland for cotton picking, or Tanganyika Lake for *dagaa* fishing. These were jobs available only to men, as their wives remained at home to care for the children. I later learned that these travels also served as a form of birth control to space out their children's births. It was shameful to have children born *kisikisi*, or like mushrooms.

With no phones back then, Makuja's departure left him and his wife Nyamalwe in a state of estrangement, devoid of communication. In actuality, this was a common occurrence amongst the villagers. When a man was absent, his family would pray for his safe return, hoping that he would find his way back home. Typically, a mindful man would reappear within a year or two. However, if he did not return after a couple of years, the community would begin to worry. After several years with no news, they would assume that he was deceased and mark his grave, conducting a symbolic burial and mourning his supposed demise. Consequently, there were graves for those who were buried and those who were presumed dead.

According to the legend, three years had passed, and Makuja had yet to return home. Nyamalwe began to mourn her husband's loss, despite her neighbors' encouragement. As time passed, Nyamalwe stopped searching for him and resigned herself to the possibility that he was gone forever. The prospect of seeing her husband again seemed improbable at best.

Nyamalwe, a mother of two, contemplated leaving her home to return to her parents. However, her love for her children kept her rooted in place, despite the weight of her grief. She had no desire to remarry, and so she saw no purpose in moving back to her parents' home. Her children were her only solace, and she resolved to stay and raise them alone.

As I mentioned before, time has an inexplicable way of working magic. Even in the midst of heartache, time can heal and soothe a tormented soul. Over time, Nyamalwe's sorrowful disposition began to transform, blending hope with uncertainty. However, as her healing merged with forgetfulness, her husband, presumed dead, knocked on the door. "Makuja is home, he is not dead!" the children shouted in outside. "Yes! He is alive. He is home," confirmed the neighbors. But with this miraculous reunion came an unforeseen calamity: Nyamalwe was six months pregnant, and tragedy was soon to follow.

At this point of the story, my mother interrupted and posed the question, "Who should be accused?" I felt as if I was jolted awake from a deep slumber. It was a test of my young judgment, and I knew it. "You're asking me?" I stammered, unsure of how to proceed. My father chimed in, "She means, between a man who vanished and a wife who couldn't wait long enough."

This situation was a classic battle of the sexes, one in which men typically emerge victorious. My father recounted how Makuja accused his wife Nyamalwe of being impatient, while she in turn blamed him for not returning. But I realized later in life that men like Makuja were not entitled to retaliate against their wives for infidelity. Makuja was consumed by a desire to devour his wife, a feeling that drove him to evict her from their home.

The village chief convened a meeting of elders to resolve the dispute before Makuja could carry out his plan. The men and women of the community also gathered in the shade at Irongeo, ready to adjudicate. The elders scolded Makuja, "it was your fault for not being present. How do you think this woman could live?" But he would not be swayed. Nyamalwe begged for his forgiveness, but Makuja was determined to send her packing.

Despite the elders' and people's admonishments, Makuja remained unyielding. He would keep Nyamalwe in his home, but he refused to accept their child. This was good enough. Cultural women do not necessarily require love to stay in a marriage. Instead, they entrust their hopes in "time," knowing that it has the power to transform conformity into consent. As long as Makuja agreed to keep Nyamalwe in his home, "time" would eventually soften his heart and he would come to accept that "the bed does not give birth to unclean" - that any child, regardless of circumstances, has the right to be considered legitimate.

But, as the Swahili proverb goes, "*Mungu sio asumani*"—God doesn't act in the same ways as humans. The following year, a young woman appeared in the village, a child strapped to her back. She strode confidently, with a clear purpose in mind. She knew exactly what she was after—her husband, the father of her child. She had sought out directions to the village and introduced herself to the chief. "I am Makuja's wife," she declared.

The scene that unfolded before the village elders was one that dripped with the drama and tension of a Shakespearean tragedy. The air was thick with confusion and disbelief as the woman, who had arrived with a child on her back, revealed that she was in fact Makuja's wife. My expression to my dad's narration echoed that of the chief's expression: one of utter perplexity as I struggled to reconcile this new information with the claims made by Makuja and his former wife Nyamalwe.

Adjusting himself from his stool, my dad continued. The truth had slowly emerged. It became clear that Makuja was married during those years of his absence. He had in fact taken another wife across the big ridge, and the two had a child. And he had kept his marriage a secret. The gravity of his actions was not lost on the elders, who demanded an explanation for his deceitful behavior. With a heavy heart, Makuja would confess to fathering the child and would accept responsibility for his actions.

In a moment of clarity, the elders turned their attention to the real victim in this saga—Nyamalwe, who had been accused of impatience and infidelity without cause. They demanded that Makuja take responsibility for his actions and right the wrongs he had committed. Despite the enormity of his transgressions, Makuja was given the opportunity to keep both wives and accept the child he had fathered outside of his marriage.

As a child, my innocent mind struggled to comprehend the societal norms that allowed a man to have multiple wives, while denying a woman the same privilege. Why was Makuja permitted to keep both his formal wife and the second woman he had secretly married, while the concept of a woman being married to two husbands seemed inconceivable? When I voiced my confusion to my father, he simply smiled in response, as if acknowledging the complexity of the situation. It was my mother, busy in the kitchen, who offered a blunt explanation. Her words tinged with a hint of bitterness. "Because HE—IS—A—MAN. A man's poo is inodorous," she declared, her tone heavy with sarcasm.

****

Despite the chaos that permeated Igengu, I couldn't help but feel like I belonged there. It was as though the village had become a part of me, and I of it. This was my first love, my first taste of pastoral life, and it held a special place in my heart. I had always heard the saying "never underestimate the power of your first love," and I could understand why. In just one year, Igengu had etched itself into my being, creating emotions and memories that would stay with me forever. Even today, Igengu remains fixed in my heart in a way that no other place could ever replicate.

After my departure, I was disheartened to learn that Mathayo, one of the worship assistants, had also left the church and remarried. Despite his outwardly decent demeanor, it was a reminder that appearances can be deceiving and that true character lies beyond what meets the eye. His previous wife had suffered a debilitating stroke during my time in the village, a condition that is often attributed to witchcraft. Sadly, instead of seeking modern medical treatment, she was left to suffer and rely solely on her husband's care.

Mathayo struggled with how to handle his wife's condition, torn between his Christian faith and the cultural beliefs surrounding illnesses. He grappled with theological questions such as whether his wife's illness was a curse from God or if she was bewitched by someone. These thoughts led him to question his own relationship with God, seeking answers to why he was facing such a difficult situation.

As a young pastor, I had tried to reassure him that God did not cause his wife's illness and that bad things can happen to good people. However, this answer often falls short of offering true solace and raises more questions than answers. It is an example of the complexity of the human condition and our search for meaning in the face of suffering.

In African belief systems, every event is often attributed to people's actions. Thus, Mathayo's struggle to reconcile his faith with his wife's illness is not uncommon. It highlights the tension between cultural and religious beliefs and the challenges of navigating these complexities.

As the turmoil continued to mount, Mathayo had sent a delegation of elders to plead his case for a second marriage due to his wife's debilitating illness. Despite his predicament, I sternly rebuked the proposition, emphasizing that it would be both unjust to his wife and a violation of his faith—a Christian principle that he once professed to hold dear. But even Christianity, with all its tenets and teachings, proved to be a mere hurdle in his path. It was a painful realization that the very thing that united us had also become a wedge driving us apart. With a heavy heart, Mathayo left the church and turned to politics. In the blink of an eye, he remarried, leaving his ailing wife to fend for herself. And in the months that followed, her lifeless body was discovered, solitary and abandoned in her home.

Suma, another devoted follower that I had recruited to serve in the church headquarters, also experienced marital woes. Despite being together for over a decade and raising children, it became clear that the smiles plastered on their faces masked a relationship that had long since soured. The aftermath was a harrowing one, leading Suma down a path of self-destruction as he turned to the bottle and the local pub for solace. Meanwhile, his estranged wife packed her bags and left Igengu for the city, leaving Suma to wallow in his misery and regret. Their marital troubles and subsequent fall from grace only added to the chaos, leaving me to question the very foundation upon which the church was built.

As if that wasn't enough, our efforts to build a new church to replace the dilapidated, muddy one were dealt a crippling blow by an earthquake that toppled the walls we had worked so tirelessly to erect. To add insult to injury, the very land that had been donated by Jeremiah for the church expansion project was now being contested, as he had suddenly changed his mind and sought to reclaim it.

The weight of disappointment pressed heavily on my shoulders as I watched everything I had labored so hard for crumble before my very eyes. The loss of trusted individuals was particularly devastating, reminding me that the church was not a product of a man's toil. I trusted that the church belongs to God and despite our shortcomings, Jesus never let his church crumble under the weight of our imperfections. It was a bitter pill to swallow but one that I had to ingest in order to detach myself emotionally from those memories. I made the decision to move on, relocating to Gumanga—a choice that was made all the more meaningful by my marriage to Deborah.

The Gumanga congregation lies not far from Igengu, and if not for the hills, a motorbike ride would take under two hours. It sits in an area mostly occupied by Muslims, and yet the community bonds among the Gumanga people exceed their religious differences. The religious life even overlaps to the point where Christians and Muslims invite each other to some of their respective worship services. It is not uncommon to see a Muslim attending Christmas or Christians invited to festivals such as Eid al-Fitr. It was no surprise, then, that my arrival was eagerly anticipated even by non-Christians.

Unlike Igengu, Gumanga was one of the oldest congregations, although its financial instability had caused many pastors to ask for a transfer. My primary ambition became building financial capacity. But what opportunities existed in this soil-barren land?

Several months after my arrival in Gumanga, a letter arrived. Its handwriting belonged to Malewo. Malewo and I have known each other since primary school, and our friendship continued into Kijota secondary school. There, we became Christian Youth leaders for all our years. Later, we formed our music band to keep ourselves out of trouble in our youth. However, we were later separated by theological colleges when I attended Kiomboi and he Mwika a year later.

As teenagers, Malewo and I were inseparable. There was no story about me that he did not know, or about him that I did not know. As we grew older, we became geared toward church activities. That was, for the most part, how we survived our teenage years and headed towards becoming pastors. Since then, Malewo and I have become like siblings.

I was a year ahead of him in finishing my theological training. Thus, when I worked at Igengu, Malewo was still completing his final year of seminary. A year later, he had been ordained and posted in a remote congregation known as Wembere. Between us, there was no means of communication. Mobile phones had emerged at this time, although they were considered a luxury, and only a select few in Tanzania could own them. For a salary like mine, buying a phone was not within the realm of dreams. Even so, cell phone towers were only present in cities, and getting a signal in the village was an entirely different matter.

To access the elusive phone, one would have to make a special visit to someone who owned one. These were typically Motorola phones with long folding-down antennas. Only one person in a hundred would own one. You would have to beg to send a text message to the owner, who must not only agree to lend you the phone but also accompany you for a mile to a specific location, be it a hill or a particular tree, where you could catch a signal bar. Even so, they would not allow you to touch the phone as you might damage it. Instead, they would text for you or hold it to your ear in case of an incoming call.

The signal strength was barely enough to download a brief text message. Even in cases of urgent communication, one could only hope that the recipient was connected to the network at the same time. If the message was not retrieved within a specific timeframe, the sender would remain in the dark about whether or not it had been received. In such circumstances, sending letters by post was the only viable option. Unfortunately, our area had no post offices, so letters had to be entrusted to public buses for delivery.

To send a letter in the absence of individual mailing boxes, one could only rely on fortuity for the bus conductor to deliver their letter to someone who knew someone who knew them. When it arrived, the letter was flung through the bus window anywhere where people gathered such as the village center. People in that area would collect it and try to figure out who is the person that the letter bears the name. For a pastor, it was somewhat easy to guess as long as the letter was cc'd to the name of the congregation, but still, that is if it got there in the first place.

In many cases, letters such as the one send by Malewo took a month or more to arrive, assuming it had survived many hands on its way, connecting one bus from another and one conductor after another as it headed towards its destination. When it eventually arrived, its envelope will have lost the ability to conceal its contents. Those who knew how to read would have read it, and those who saw something of value in it would have removed it from the envelope. Regardless of these challenges, Malewo and I kept writing to each other very often, sharing our sentiments.

In his latest congregation, Malewo was confronted with a marital conundrum. "Bro," he started his letter, a colloquial term for "brother." "A few weeks ago, a married woman came to me in distress. She was a woman of integrity and godliness who had been married for six years but had not been blessed with children. As she knocked on my office door, I sensed the deep sadness that had consumed her for far too long. 'Pastor,' she said, her eyes brimming with tears, 'how can you help me?' I felt her pain acutely, even as I struggled to understand the root of her sorrow."

The woman poured out her heart to Malewo, revealing how she and her husband had been attempting to conceive for six years without success, despite engaging in all manner of prayer chains. Despite their efforts, her in-laws and relatives' pressure continued to mount, as they had tried every hospital without success. The last doctor they visited had delivered a bleak diagnosis, and the woman felt like she had failed as a wife and a woman. "I feel like people think I'm not enough of a woman," she confided in Malewo. "The entire village is against me," she added.

Compounding their misery, the husband was the only son in the family, adding to the pressure on them to produce an heir. He struggled to reconcile his childless marriage with his devout Christian faith. However, that wasn't the reason why the woman had come to Malewo.

"My problem is more significant than that, Pastor!" she exclaimed. "My younger sister, who I had invited to stay with me, is pregnant. Yes, I know she's a grown woman and has her own life, but I wish it were that simple," she lamented. "I can hardly believe it. I don't even know how to explain it," she sobbed, wiping her tears away. "Anyway, I confronted her about it, but she refused to tell me who the father of her child was. My parents are furious and demand to know. It took me a long time to persuade her to reveal the truth to me, and when she finally did, I regretted asking. Because the truth is that the pregnancy is my husband's, my own spouse. I can't believe this!" She broke down into tears again.

The woman was inconsolable, and her tears flowed like a raging river. She felt betrayed by her own flesh and blood, and the guilt of having asked her sister about the pregnancy weighed heavily on her. Malewo listened attentively, his heart filled with empathy for the woman's plight.

As the woman continued to pour out her heart, Malewo realized that he was dealing with a delicate situation that required both wisdom and tact. He knew that the woman's faith was paramount to her, and he needed to address the issue with a gentle yet firm hand. Malewo offered a comforting shoulder to the woman as he pondered how to navigate the choppy waters of her marital predicament.

As Malewo recounted the woman's tale, he pondered the complexity of the situation at hand. The woman had discovered her husband's infidelity, yet forgiveness seemed out of reach. Her sister's pregnancy was only a reminder of her husband's betrayal, adding to her six years of the emotional turmoil. In certain Tanzanian traditions, such a transgression would require the man to marry the woman he impregnated. However, given the couple's Christian faith, such an outcome was not so simple.

As Malewo grappled with the gravity of the matter, he considered the potential solutions with trepidation. Should he advise the pregnant sister to have an abortion to protect the marriage, or should he encourage the wife to divorce her husband so that he could marry his sister-in-law? Abortion was not an option from a pastor and yet, the latter option seemed shameful and impractical, given the taboo surrounding such a union. The woman's love for her husband only added to the complexity of the situation.

Malewo's thoughts were consumed with questions that had no easy answers. Then, there was a theological side of the matter. Could the man's confession and repentance ever be enough to heal the wounds he had inflicted? Was the woman's love enough to overcome the hurt and betrayal she had experienced? Would the woman resort to suicide if the marriage ended in divorce? These questions swirled around Malewo's mind as he wrote, seeking guidance and wisdom to untangle this intricate web of emotions and traditions.

As I read Malewo's letter, I couldn't help but feel a knot form in my stomach. It was like a tangled web of tradition, religion, and morality, all intersecting in a way that left everyone trapped. The woman's husband had strayed, and now their lives were caught in a snare of consequences. All of our lives were currently caught in the uncertainty.

I sensed the dark cloud loomed over them, threatening to burst at any moment. Malewo could feel the weight of it pressing down on him, just as the woman must have felt the weight of shame and betrayal. It was like a heavy burden that they were all forced to carry, no matter how unfair or unjust it seemed.

As I read his words, I couldn't help but think of the ancient Greek myth of King Oedipus. Like Oedipus, the woman's husband had committed such a grave sin and now found himself caught in a web of guilt and shame. And like Oedipus, the consequences of his actions would ripple through the lives of those around him, leaving a trail of destruction in their wake.

But Malewo knew that this was no myth, no story from a distant past. This was real life, and the choices they made would have real consequences. Could the man's confession and repentance ever be enough to heal the wounds he had inflicted? Was the woman's love enough to overcome the hurt and betrayal she had experienced? Would the woman resort to suicide if the marriage ended in divorce? These questions repeated in Malewo's mind again and again as he wrote to me, seeking wisdom from a clueless friend.

VII

-

"Let him marry another wife"

—A woman's comment

—

MALEWO, WITH A HEAVY heart, continued to compose his letter to seek counsel on another conundrum that faced a couple whose dreams of union were marred by a single positive test result for HIV. He had registered a wedding, and a couple were required to undergo testing as a standard procedure. To his dismay, the man tested positive, while the woman was negative. Despite his advice against proceeding with the marriage, they were adamant about their love and faith in God. Malewo urged them to reconsider, but they defied his warnings. The woman, being "born again," was so convinced that love would conquer all and their faith would see them through. Malewo's struggle was one of conviction versus compassion, as he grappled with the complexity of reconciling the couple's fervent beliefs with the harsh reality of the virus.

He gave them more time to consider. Although in reality, he needed that time to think through the situation. It was during this time that he penned to me, wondering if there was a higher power to whom he could appeal for guidance on this issue, for he felt that he was caught in a tug-of-war between the couple's hopeful promises and his own misgivings about the man's integrity. Despite his reluctance to pass judgment, Malewo could not deny his growing mistrust of the man, who he believed was concealing promiscuous behavior. He wished he could impart this truth to the bride-to-be, but her unwavering faith rendered her impervious to his words of caution.

In time, Malewo would learn that the couple decided to go ahead with their marriage, only for it to unravel in a few short months. The wife, whose faith had been her guiding light, would find herself betrayed as she eventually learned that her once "God-fearing" husband was a philanderer. Faith can be ironic. What was once an unshakable force became a cruel twist of fate, leaving her vulnerable to the very thing she had hoped to evade. However, her revelation was too late, for by then, she had contracted the virus too. This was a bitter reminder that love is not always enough.

Malewo's letter arrived with a tinge of irony as I had just recently encountered a similar case in one of Gumanga's sub-congregations. In Tanzania, congregations comprise multiple churches, forming an administrative area that can span vast distances. These churches are overseen by "evangelists," who assist with various responsibilities but are limited on what they can perform, for example pastoral services like baptism or communion, which require a pastor's presence. For these services, the pastor must be there.

During my one of these visits, the evangelist had informed me of a couple in need of pastoral care. I made a note for myself to attend the case. After the worship, I sat on the dusty church pew, as there was no office. Listening to the couple's account of their situation, I couldn't help but feel a pang of sympathy for their plight.

They had been married for nine years or so if I remember correctly and had a daughter, but the wife's recent illness had led them on a tumultuous journey. The husband was the one who nervously started the conversation, "We have a problem, pastor!" His wife gazed at the dusty floor in silence. "Please, do tell," I responded. The husband hesitated before continuing, "My wife has fallen very ill recently. We initially suspected malaria but numerous visits to dispensaries yielded no relief. It was only after a trip to Hydom hospital and a blood test that we discovered she was HIV positive." "HIV," I repeated with shock. The man, in a quivering voice, continued to recount the news in detail, while his wife's gaze maintained the fixed position on the ground.

The memory of that day remains vivid in my mind, as if frozen in time. The gentle flicker of the adobe church's dimmed light cast an amber glow, like a beacon guiding lost souls through the labyrinth of their own melancholy. The dust danced in the air, swirling and twirling in a mournful waltz, as if mourning the sadness that permeated the space. It coated every surface like a thick veil, concealing the vibrancy of hope that once filled our churchly moods. In moments like these, life changes its meaning so fast.

The brief silence broke among us. Outside, the calls of lonely birds echoed through our silence like a mournful requiem, their melancholic notes piercing the heavy atmosphere within us. The very air had become imbued with a palpable sense of desolation and grief, suffocating all our faith beneath its weight.

I took a far-fetched breath, to attempt to ease the couple's burden. What I had heard was the story that echoed the intricacies of life's web, woven with threads of hopelessness, despair, and unexpected turns. In every couple's tone, the fragility of our humanness was vivid—not a good reminder, but life's trials often defy our understanding and control. I was there, supposedly, to bring the solution, but the burden of their predicament rested heavily on my novice pastoral shoulders. I adjusted myself on an uncomfortable pew, knowing that the couple's fate was now left in the hands of an unyielding disease.

I looked at the man before to create a space for him to continue. He was fraught with confusion, his voice unsteady as he spoke. "Honestly, we were baffled—I was very confused. And we are still at a loss as to how it happened—how she contracted HIV . . ." He trailed off uncertainly. "I asked her about it but she claimed not to know," he continued uninterrupted. "Not that I don't trust her—I do—and yet, I don't comprehend. As a human, I am allowed to have doubts. Could she have strayed outside our marriage? Where could she have contracted it? How could this have happened? I don't believe she had an affair, but my mind is a maelstrom of confusion."

"I am deeply sorry to hear this," I murmured sympathetically as the man began became somber.

The air around us continued to grow thicker. Every breath we took, and every droplet of saliva that escaped our lips, echoed through the empty expanse of the deserted building. We were trapped in a world of our own sadness, each lost in our own isolated thoughts, pondering the very value of our existence.

The man recollected and continued, "Well, we have consulted with the doctor about it—how it could have happened, that is. He suggested that there are many ways in which she might have contracted it. She may have contracted it when she underwent a blood transfusion during her pregnancy of our daughter. Or perhaps she may have contracted it during her first marriage, though that was over ten years ago. Can that be possible? I don't know, I really don't know," he concluded, taking a pause.

The very same building that one hour ago heralded the brightest of all hopes in the world now held us prisoners of uncertainty and despair. We were standing on the edge of a precipice, undoing every sermon that we held dearly. I took a deep breath, searching for the words to ease their despair and provide comfort. Meanwhile, the wife sat beside the man quietly, her tears streaming down her face, but with a greater sense of composure than her husband. As time went on, her presence seemed to fade into the background like a shadow cast by the light of her anguish, as her husband spoke on her behalf.

"Well, I suppose it doesn't matter how it happened now . . . whatever the cause, the fact is that she is sick. That's why we came to you, Pastor. What should I do?" The man asked, his concern palpable.

I adjusted myself on a concrete pew to prepare a response for what I had just heard. As I gazed at the troubled man before me, I could see nothing but his ego. Yet I refrained from making a hasty judgement. "These were not issues that were covered in theology school," I thought to myself. After all, I had only been married for a few months. How could I possibly know how to address these marital issues?

As I tried to form a response, my mind frantically searched for a Bible verse to start the conversation with, but none came to mind. This young counselor definitely needed more time to think, but there was no time. Before I could say anything, the man interrupted with a loaded question, "I mean, she is my wife, but how can we live as husband and wife?" His implication was clear: how would they have sex?

"Sex, you mean?" I asked to confirm.

"Yes, pastor," he responded honestly but shyly.

"Have you considered other means?" I asked, hoping to ease the tension.

"You mean . . . no," he replied, "I'm afraid to use condoms. I've heard they're not safe. And besides, condoms cost money, and our local shops don't even sell them." His statement rang true. It was unlikely that one would find condoms in the small kiosks that lined the village streets.

"How do you want me to help then?" I inquired, my mind racing to find a solution.

"Save my life, pastor. I don't want to die," the man pleaded.

I knew what he meant. "When you say 'save my life,' what do you mean?" I asked, trying to gauge the depth of the issue.

At this point, the woman spoke up, her voice heavy with sorrow. "Let him marry another wife, Pastor."

I jumped to a premature conclusion. "You mean you want to divorce your wife?"

"No," the man said, "we were thinking maybe he could be allowed to get married to a second wife because of . . . other things, you know. Since I can no longer offer him . . ." The woman trailed off, her sincerity etched on her face.

As I contemplated their request, I glanced over at their six-year-old child playing near the church mud pews. My heart ached as I looked back at the woman, left with nothing but to beg for her husband's sexual needs. "Let him marry another wife," replayed in my mind. I couldn't help but wonder "how?"

An empty silence broke between us. For a moment, I lost myself in a "what if" scenario as I stepped into the man's shoes, allowing myself to be consumed by his anguish. "What would I do if I were in his position?" I wondered. Would I seek comfort in another woman's arms or continue living in a sexless marriage? My thoughts darted back and forth like a pendulum, from the man to the woman and then back to me. "Perhaps this man is praying for his wife's demise so he can be free," I speculated, my gaze locked unfairly on him. But then, as if struck by a sudden epiphany, I turned the tables. "What if the roles were reversed?" I mused, my mind racing with possibilities. "Would this woman have done the same to her husband?" I interrogated myself, while the couple's request hung precariously in the air.

I contemplated the depth of the man's suffering. My mind couldn't help but ponder on the magnitude of his sacrifice. He deserved credit, I reckoned, for standing by his wife through thick and thin, for attempting to find a solution together. Another man, given the same set of circumstances, would have abandoned his spouse or sought comfort in the arms of a stranger. But this man had at least taken the time to seek "pastoral" advice, to ask for a "favor," as he put it. If only I could give him the answer he sought.

"Why do you speak of yourself? Why do you use 'I'?" I asked, my annoyance palpable. "Why not think of 'us,' both of you? Or even think of your child? If the tables were turned, and you were the one suffering, would you ask me to let your wife marry another man?" I prodded, hoping to make him see the flaws in his thinking.

"No, Pastor, I wouldn't," he responded sheepishly, "but this is different . . . you know."

"Different—how different?" I asked in a rebuking manner, my voice laced with a touch of impatience. "Think about why you married her. Was it solely for sex? You should be thanking God that he has protected you thus far. Remember when you both didn't know she had HIV? I'm surprised you don't believe that was a miracle!" I lectured him, feeling as if I was slipping into the role of a moralistic zealot. But the man's request was too great, too all-encompassing for him to see reason. His eyes, dark and haunted, implored me to find a practical solution, any solution, and yet I failed him.

I had come to realize that sometimes our tendency to over-spiritualize people's experiences only serves to further complicate their problems. I couldn't help but wonder if that was exactly what I had done during this encounter with a struggling couple. Despite my good intentions, I had failed to provide any practical solutions for their marital issues, resorting instead to simplistic phrases like "trust in God", "seek medical advice," and "use condoms."

Ahead of me was an arduous hour cycling on a sandy pavement, competing with the setting sun casting an orange glow quietly behind *staferi* trees. The day had started beautifully but had turned bleak. The bushy road of Gumanga was eerily silent, and my mind was plagued with questions.

Would the man succumb to his desires and cheat on his wife, leaving her to die alone like Mathayo had done in Igengu? Would he decide to take another wife, abandoning his sickly spouse to die? And what of the wife's feelings towards my words—had I made myself clear when I told him he could not remarry until death?

Lost in my thoughts, as I rode my old Phoenix bicycle through the bushy roads of Gumanga. I couldn't shake off the feeling that my words had fallen short. Was the use of condoms even practical in this remote village, where even a matchstick was limited? Even if they were, would the couple be able to afford them over the course of their marriage? And most importantly, was there any other practical answer I could have offered?

I contemplated the complexities of human nature and the nuances of marital issues. Love, Christian ethics, human rights, sexuality—all of these concepts swirled around in my mind, leading me to a place of emotional exhaustion and unobservable consequences.

I continued my ride through the sandy cow paths of the desolate village, my thoughts engulfed in the heavy burden of unaddressed inquiries. However, I later came to the conclusion that my role as a pastor was probably not to provide all the answers, but rather to offer a listening ear and a guiding voice. And so, I had asked the couple to go home and think about their situation before coming back to me with their final decision. But as the months passed by and they never returned, I couldn't help but wonder what they had chosen.

Should I have followed up with them? Perhaps. But even years later, as I think back to that encounter, I am reminded of the complexities of this case and the limitations of my ability to solve their problem. The challenges of modern-day marriage in a traditional society like Gumanga continue to cast a shadow over my conscience. In the face of such failure, it is easy to feel inadequate, as if my words were nothing more than platitudes.

****

There was another poignant case in Igengu that shared similar sentiments with the one above. This involved Neema, a woman in the prime of her life, who had weathered the tumultuous storm of marital abandonment. When she visited me, Neema's eyes were like pools of sadness, reflecting the deep frustration. She told me that she was married, although the husband had left her without a trace, leaving behind only the shattered remnants of their once-happy life.

Back then, the village was grappling with the unforgiving grip of adversity. In an effort to keep their heads above water, Neema and her husband had come to an agreement—the man would set out on a quest for gainful employment in the city to provide for their loved ones. However, little did they know that the search would be akin to looking for a needle in a haystack.

The couple had two children, a girl and a boy, who were the beacons of hope in Neema's desolate world. It had been almost four years now since her husband left the Gumanga area without any word of his whereabouts or fate. For the wife, the burden of single motherhood was weighing heavy, although carried with stoic resilience.

"I don't know what got him. I do not know if he is dead or alive," she said, her voice trailing off into a wistful sigh. "I really don't know—and I am tired of taking care of the children alone," she confessed, her words like a lamentation, a mournful song of a soul caught in the web of marital disillusionment and societal constraints.

Neema implored me to provide her with a letter of referral so that she could initiate divorce proceedings, or alternatively, to ascertain if she could be allowed to remarry. It may seem puzzling why a pastor would be involved in the process of obtaining a divorce. However, in Tanzania, all marriages are governed by the country's legal framework, and the church, as a registered institution, conducts marriage ceremonies in compliance with the relevant laws and directives. Following an application for legal certification, a pastor is authorized to officiate at wedding services.

If a marriage does come to an end, especially one that was held in church, the court often requests some sort of background of the problem from the church to process the divorce, a process akin to the probing of a wound, a search for the source of the pain. This means a letter that gave some context on how the matter had been handled internally by the church. A couple that bypassed the church and went straight to court were likely to be sent back to the church by the court, a testament to the significance of the institution in the fabric of society. I wondered whether this procedure was in the law or was just a court's tradition, a reflection of the interplay of tradition and modernity, of the old and the new.

Therefore, the arduous process of divorce in Tanzanian churches involved a rigorous procedure. First, the couple had to undergo a thorough assessment by the church council, which was often a daunting experience that required immense emotional strength. If this attempt failed to reconcile the couple, the pastor would have to issue a referral letter to the court, which would determine the fate of the marriage. Thus, the pastor's letter was the final seal in the divorce process, marking the end of a tumultuous journey for the couple.

Despite the lack of clear church policy on divorce, Tanzanian churches held a steadfast belief that "two will become one flesh . . . they are no longer two, but one flesh . . . what God has joined together, let man not separate." This meant that once a couple was married, they were bound by a sacred covenant that could not be dissolved, even when their relationship was plagued by insurmountable challenges.

In the church that I served, divorce was essentially deemed impossible, with exceptions made only in rare circumstances. For instance, a person could remarry only after their recorded reasons for the breakup of their first marriage had been evaluated by the church. However, this was an unwritten policy that had to be navigated delicately. The church held the view that only the "victim" of the divorce, rather than the "initiator," could remarry.

In other words, the person who filed for divorce was deemed responsible for the breakdown of the marriage. This created a predicament for individuals who had initiated the divorce for genuine reasons but were nonetheless considered at fault by the church. These individuals were deemed unfit for church membership and could not remarry within the church. It was a harsh reality that left many feeling ostracized from their faith community.

The church's unwritten policy regarding divorce placed limitations on those who initiated or were a party to a divorce. Even if they remained unmarried, their access to certain spiritual services, such as participating in the holy communion or holding church leadership positions, would be curtailed. Essentially, only the recipient of the divorce order was deemed to be the victim and considered innocent of any wrongdoing, allowing them to remarry if they so desired. While it may have been possible for the opposite to be true, this was not accounted for in the rule.

However, the policy contained several loopholes, one of which I witnessed firsthand. Men like Jacob, who were abusive to their wives, often portrayed themselves as good in the eyes of the public, despite mistreating their wives to the point where they could no longer endure it and seek a divorce. The abuser would then feign affection and profess his love for his wife, refusing to initiate a divorce since he did not consider himself the victim. Instead, the wife would file for divorce, and as a result, the church would often blame her for lacking endurance and either excommunicate her or prohibit her from remarrying. Meanwhile, the abuser would be left free to continue with his harmful behavior.

Such flawed policies were riddled with challenges, and Neema's case was a perfect example. She had initiated divorce in the absence of her husband, and since he had left her, it was reasonable to consider Neema the victim according to marriage laws. However, for the church, I had to prove that her husband was either deceased or married to another woman. Unfortunately, the man was nowhere to be found, and I faced the challenge of establishing his fate. Furthermore, he had left before the advent of mobile phones, and nobody knew if he had died or remarried. Despite all this, Neema still professed love for her husband, referring to him as a good man. The dilemma was evident—where had he disappeared to, and for how long?

There were a few challenges that made the situation even more heart-wrenching. When the man left, there were no mobile phones to bridge the distance between him and his family. He did not just disappear into the night; it was a mutual decision for him to travel, in the hopes of finding a better life and returning to his loved ones. However, as time went on, no one knew for certain where he was, or even if he was still alive. Neema, in her own words, still loved him, despite the years that had passed. "He was a good man," she pointed out. "We have children together, but where is he now—for all these years?" It was a dilemma that weighed heavily on her heart.

As I mentioned earlier, in the old days, men from the village would often leave their families behind and venture out to other places in search of a better life. Some would travel to the mines, others to work in plantations or in the jungle to herd cows. Some men disappeared to Magugu onions farms or to Mererani for Tanzanite mining. My dad would often regale us with tales of his trips to Sukuma land to harvest cotton, while my mom was left behind for a whole year. His village fellows would leave for Muria lake to produce salt or to Mpwani to catch fish. The expectation was that whoever left their family behind for these expeditions would always come back, like a homing pigeon returning to its nest.

Some men returned home to their families after a year or two, while others took five years or more. With no mail addresses or phones to communicate, wives and children were left with only their extended families and the hope that their fathers would return as long as they were alive. "*Igutambaa ghunto igusuka*," people would always say, meaning "the bird flies high in the sky, but its destiny is on the land." The implication was that any man in a good mind would always return home to his family.

But did every man come back? The answer is no. Some men did return, but others were lost to hardship, illness, or even the allure of city life and its temptations. In Haji's case, my cousin, he had left many years ago before I was born and never came back. His parents have since passed away, and still, he has not come back. Rumors abounded that he had fallen prey to alcoholism. The tragic fate may be running in the family; we buried his younger brother years ago for the same reason, and the other one who also traveled to Magugu is heading down the same path. Anyhow!

It is said that Haji's whereabouts remain a mystery to his family, though some claim to have seen him leading a difficult life toiling in rice plantations and squandering his earnings on local brews. Reflecting on

Haji's circumstances, I couldn't help but wonder if Neema's own husband had succumbed to a similar fate, drowning in the bottle or remarrying. Could there be a legitimate explanation for his absence, one that precluded his return to his loved ones?

As Neema and I delved into these possibilities, I realized I was only making things more difficult for her. "Should we entertain the possibility that your husband has passed away or remarried?" I asked, searching for her perspective. "What if he's locked up in jail with no one to bail him out? What if he shows up one day with a legitimate reason, only to find that you've moved on . . . would you cast him aside? And what about your children if he returned today?" Even as I posed these senseless questions, I was keenly aware of my own inability to answer them. As for Neema, she was left in a state of limbo, unsure of whether her husband was alive, dead, or had remarried. Despite the passage of time and the lack of any concrete information, her love of him was still visible on her face. Somehow her own imagination had been unable to let go of the hope that he would one day return to her and their children, and yet she was tired of waiting. How long could one be expected to wait for a loved one's return?

As I pondered on this, I realized the insidious nature of gender inequality that still pervaded our society. The burden of waiting, of holding onto hope, of being faithful, was placed solely on the woman. It was as if the man's desires and needs were more important than the woman's and that she was merely an accessory to his life. After reflecting deeply, I suggested that Neema return home to reflect on all the possibilities we had discussed. I advised her to take her time and return to me when she was ready to take the next step. Neema agreed to this and left my office, but she never returned to me before I left Gumanga.

It was only after Neema left that I realized the extent of my privilege as a man. These incidents also exposed my shortcomings as a pastor. I asked myself a simple yet poignant question: "Would a man wait for this long?" The answer was unequivocally "No." No man in our society would endure such a lengthy separation from his wife without seeking comfort elsewhere. If a man would not wait, then why should Neema be subjected to such a punishment just because she was a woman?

VIII

-

"Because He Is a man"

—My mother's comment

—

Men, in their desires, cannot be told to wait. Because they are men. Their unbridled passions and their persistent libidos do not wane with age. Their desires are uncontrolled and can be likened to an uncovered spear, always ready to penetrate any opening or flesh. The conviction of perpetuity that often characterizes the male psyche in our cultural milieu leads many men to believe themselves exempt from the effects of temporal progression. They choose to marry who they want and divorce who they are tired of. They know how to have more than how to keep. They are born "men." They are innately endowed to preside over the domain of marriage and divorce, or at least that's what I felt under the influence of Gumanga.

Malewo's letter did not return with any reasonable advice, but it triggered a series of reflections on manhood. I found myself delving into memories, and one that immediately came to mind was about Juma, a distant relative who shared the same grandparents with my father. According to our culture, I would refer to Juma as "baba mkubwa," which means senior father, and he would address me as his son. Traditionally, all my father's immediate or distant brothers would be referred to as my 'fathers,' their wives as my mothers, and their children as my siblings. The same applied to my mother's sisters; they were my senior or junior mothers.

It had been a while since I last saw Juma, who had retired from serving in the army, as my father had told me. One day, while walking back from the farm with my father, we spotted him from a distance. I had no idea that he had returned from his last post until that moment. Juma was my father's age, and all his children had grown up, with his youngest child about my age. As we approached him, I noticed an unfamiliar young woman by his side. I could not immediately speculate on their relationship, but I was certain that she was not one of his children as I knew them all. Later, I came to learn that her name was Amina.

My father had caught sight of them before they could reach us. In Arimi culture, such a meeting demands a *sayu*, a formal and detailed exchange of pleasantries that encompasses all that has happened since the last time the parties met. As my father and Juma shook hands, the latter inquired about my identity with an air of unfamiliarity. "Have you forgotten him? This is your son—Kaghondi," my father responded with a beaming smile, introducing me by my traditional name. "Ah, look at him," Juma exclaimed with paternal pride. "He has grown into a full man!" he exclaimed with an infectious smile, addressing me as his "father," a nod to our cultural tradition where an inherited name confers fatherhood upon the recipient.

I extended my right hand to shake his, reciprocating the warmth of his greeting with a respectful "*shikamoo*." He beamed at me, then gestured to the young woman by his side. "And this is your mother," he said, introducing me to Amina. It was only then that I realized she was Juma's new wife. Amina was indeed my "mother" in the traditional sense, but her youthful appearance made it difficult for me to reconcile the idea of addressing her with the customary greeting of *shikamoo*. It was a paradoxical situation— she deserved the respect of a mother but her age was incongruous with the role. My mind was filled with a torrent of questions and emptiness, trying to make sense of the situation before me. How was I supposed to reconcile the cultural expectations of showing respect to "my mother" when she was almost my contemporary in age? And if I was roughly seventeen at the time, how old could Amina be? I was left with a feeling of confusion and disorientation, as if a familiar landscape had suddenly shifted and become unrecognizable.

As I observed the young woman, a sense of pity and compassion overwhelmed me. Her timid insecure demeanor and inability to meet my gaze conveyed her vulnerability and naivety. I couldn't help but feel empathy for her as we all struggled to navigate the complexities of the social norms placed upon us. The awkward silence hung between us. The moment palpable and uncomfortable, like a heavy cloak swallowing us both.

As my father and Juma exchanged pleasantries, the two of us remained trapped in an awkward silence. In that moment, I found myself at a loss for words, my tongue twisting and turning in a strange and uncomfortable dance. I observed the young woman's timid disposition, her eyes casting downward and her words stilted, as if meant to discourage my attempt to address her properly.

As we made our way back home, my mind was consumed by a torrent of questions. How could such a young woman be wedded to a man so much older than her father? What had led her to enter into such an unconventional marriage?

My father, ever perceptive, could sense my distress and sought to ease my concerns. He broached the topic delicately, his tone heavy with the weight of the story he was about to tell. In his words, I could sense the presence of a long and complex narrative waiting to be revealed.

It was as if he needed to brace himself for what he was about to say. With a solemn and deliberate pause, he cleared his throat, and expelled a fragment of his toothbrush made from tree bark, before he finally divulged the truth behind Juma's recent nuptials. The revelation was delivered with a gravity that spoke of a deeper story behind the seemingly scandalous union.

"That girl you saw," he finally began, "is Juma's new wife. They got married a few months ago." I was taken aback by this revelation, struggling to comprehend how such a young and shy girl could be married to a man who tripled her age. "But how is that possible?" I demanded, my frustration palpable. "Amina is just a girl. Did she fall in love with that man?" I asked, impatient for answers.

"It's complicated," my father sighed, pausing again as if trying to gather his thoughts. He adjusted his shoulder and wiped something on his left ear before continuing. "You see, your father has taken up the mantle of a traditional healer or witch doctor, as some call it. In these days, he spends his days collecting rocks and herbs, and we fear that he has lost his mind. We suspect that years of military service have taken a toll on his brain, and he has spiraled into madness. His mental state is questionable at best, and as a result, his entire family has abandoned him—his children, his wife, all gone."

My father's words were articulate but carried a suspense that left me hung heavily in the air. I listened intently, feeling a mix of emotions churning inside me—confusion, frustration, and a deep sadness. I could not help but feel a sense of curiosity about Juma's new wife and the circumstances that led to their marriage.

With a deep sigh, my father continued: "So he is a doctor, if you will." Dad shook his head, and continued in an improvisatory manner, his eyes clouded with revulsion. "His house is now a cluttered den, filled with what he calls 'medicine.' He professes to have been bestowed with divine power to heal incurable diseases and banish demons, and he promises to bring *kismati* (luck) to those in search of love. His behavior has grown increasingly erratic, so much so that all of us are not sure how to tolerate his antics."

"But what of Amina?" I interrupted.

"Ah, yes," my father paused, as if he had forgot about the subject. "That girl!" He paused again. "A few months ago, this young woman was his patient. Her parents had brought her to Juma, claiming she would fall unconscious and be overtaken by spells. Juma diagnosed it as a sign of "evil spirits" and began treating her with his "medicine." She stayed with him for a while, taking his herbs and undergoing his rituals. Some days, she would feel better, but her symptoms always returned. This went on for some time until her parents finally took her back home, only to see her fall ill again."

I couldn't help but feel angry. The image of Juma's cluttered house filled with his so-called "medicine" and bizarre rituals lingered in my mind. It was clear that this young woman had suffered greatly, and I couldn't imagine the desperation her parents must have felt to seek out Juma's help. But I still couldn't comprehend how she ended up how she ended up with him to be cured or as his wife.

"And?"

"And after Amina stayed with Juma for several months, the *muvie wa mahuka*—medical expenses—skyrocketed to exorbitant heights. Juma demanded that Amina's parents pay a hefty sum of money to redeem their daughter, a cost they couldn't possibly afford."

"Was she even cured?" I interjected, my curiosity piqued.

"Unfortunately, no," my father sighed. "Juma decided to keep her captive until her parents paid the full bill. And each day, he added even more to the already exorbitant cost, until he claimed Amina as his wife in compensation. He claimed that by marrying her, he could provide her with the personal care she needed for her problems."

"And her parents agreed to this?" I asked incredulously.

"No, they did not agree," my father responded. "But they had no choice. Juma had threatened to summon the evil spirits that he claimed were plaguing their daughter if they refused. They were powerless in the face of his threats."

"And nothing has been done about it?" I asked, my frustration mounting.

My father let out a wry laugh. "What do you do, son? A man's poo is inodorous."

The parable "a man's poo is inodorous" echoed in my mind. "This man is walking free with an underage girl simply because he is a man," I said to myself. I couldn't understand how a man nearly sixty years old could marry a young woman who was not even close in age to his youngest child. How could such an injustice occur in the modern world, and why had no one intervened to stop it?

****

Juma's reprehensible behavior haunted me for years, and even now, in a supposedly civilized society, such abhorrent acts persist. Despite Tanzania's laws prohibiting such practices, they continue to thrive, with men often operating above the law, immune to the consequences of their sexual misconduct. Our culture has fostered a sense of entitlement in men, making them believe they are above reproach. Women, on the other hand, are left with no recourse but to resign themselves to fate.

It is a lesson I learned firsthand, through the story of Mkulima, a respected Christian in our community and my childhood role model. Married with children, Mkulima was a skilled veterinarian whose work was nothing short of mesmerizing to a teenage me. He was the man our livestock relied on for survival, his needle tip the arbiter of life and death for our cattle. Even the most pesky of pests—the cotton flea hopper, the clouded plant bug, and the Verde plant bug in our cotton fields—cowered before him, unable to evade his insecticides.

Mkulima was a paragon of his time. Amidst children frolicking, I watched him with rapt admiration. I longed to emulate him, to be associated with his name. Wherever he went, I trailed closely behind, mesmerized by the way he expertly injected medicine into cows' thighs or diagnosed the quality of butchered meat. His technique was a thing of beauty, and when he mixed insecticides, which we referred to as "poison," I yearned for the chance to carry his pump like a backpack. As he added water to the spray tank, I was there, hovering eagerly at his side, hoping he would let me hold the nozzle. I accompanied him on his professional rounds throughout the village, feeling as though I were transported to heaven with each moment spent in his company.

He was one of the few educated people in our village. A high-class, erudite man, who, when he was drunk, would forget all his mother tongue and Swahili and speak only English. And when he spoke, he would purse his lips in a British style, and all the vocabulary that came out was accompanied by his own translation. In a society where education was a rare commodity, his intellect was beyond heavens. He was one of the remaining products of colonial middle schools, whose education had instilled in him a deep sense of the supremacy of the English language. In the village, men like him could pour themselves a local beer from anyone's gourd, their status and education granting them such privileges.

I was acquainted with Mkulima's children, whom I shared a classroom with during my primary school years. However, my heart was heavy with envy when I beheld their polished sneakers, a far cry from my unadorned feet which didn't feel the comfort of sandals until I reached high school. My own notebooks were carried in a tattered plastic bag, but Mkulima's offspring had backpacks that were nothing short of fancy. Moreover, their command of proper Swahili was something to marvel at, unlike some of us who struggled to disentangle it from our native tongues.

Those who knew Mkulima intimately, such as my parents, often attributed his achievements to his wife. She was a gentle and kind-hearted soul, one of those individuals known as "*hawana makuu*" in Swahili, signifying a lack of arrogance. Despite the family's status, Mkulima's wife never exalted herself nor looked down on others. She was the epitome of godliness, having grown up in a destitute family, weathering many hardships in her lifetime. When she married Mkulima, she worked tirelessly on the farm and supported him in attending college. Even when he was away, she dutifully sent him money to pay his tuition fees and managed the household finances by selling their crops. In essence, she was the driving force behind the family's upward trajectory, without whom Mkulima's hubris and recklessness would have proven to be insurmountable obstacles.

Mkulima's rise to success was meteoric. With the earnings from their hard work, he and his wife acquired a vast tract of land and erected a magnificent, modern home. Theirs was the only contemporary residence in the village, and Mkulima's fame and fortune extended far beyond the borders of Mtinko. They amassed an impressive array of assets including hundreds of cows, oxen carts, and a motorbike.

However, as Arimi astutely observed, wealth can be as transient as a rat's cotton tail—appearing full, but easily detachable. The Kiswahili proverb *"ngoma ikivuma sana hupasuka"*—a drum that sounds too loud will soon burst—rang true for Mkulima as well. His star had reached its zenith, but it was now dimming fast, as the dust of the sky began to shroud it. While many would attribute his downfall to the corrupting influence of money, I tend to blame it on remembrance. It was his failure to remember where he came from that led to his undoing.

Memory is everything. Memory is that vital thread that provides the bridge between recollection and presence and serves as a bulwark against forgetfulness and ignorance. The gap between forgetfulness and ignorance is closed by memories. Sadly, Mkulima had lost his connection to his past due to his arrogance. He has become a disciple of forgetfulness, and his success and popularity silenced the enactments of remembrance. The rationality that had guided him in the past was now a distant memory, and he had lost sight of himself in what he believed to be "the man." My people said, "his money begun to scratch in his pockets," meaning that his wealth had gone to his head.

Over time, "the man" began to see elderliness in his wife. He begun to view her with disdain, finding her appearance unappealing and outdated. In his hubris, he believed he deserved a younger woman. When he was intoxicated, he would denigrate the beauty of his lifelong companion who had endured his bodily odors and premature ejaculations for over a quarter century. His arrogance only intensified, and his spouse's attraction to him dwindled. On several occasions, he nearly failed to return home, only to blame his wife for not bothering to look after him.

Despite her warnings, he obstinately persisted. His children lamented, yet their admonitions fell on deaf ears, in the manner of the Swahili proverb, "words enter one ear and exit the other." For the villagers, who relished the spectacle of a *muhuve* tree falling, witnessing the decline of a wealthy man was particularly enthralling. Alas, Mkulima was hurtling towards his downfall at a precipitous pace, rapidly shedding his once-mighty wings. It was a tragic sight to behold, but few things gratified the poor villagers more than observing a formerly prosperous individual plunging into destitution due to his own arrogance. Regrettably, Mkulima was oblivious to his impending doom.

His manliness was swallowing him, and he was blindfolded from it. His memories became distant echoes drowned out by his ego. As the Waswahili proverb states, "*Sikio la kufa halisikii dawa*"—a dying ear never hears of the medicine, and the Arimi people add, "*Mwenda gurungu atyu-tangwaa*"—the person who is headed to gods is unstoppable. Despite being alive, Mkulima was like a dying ear and a man on the path to the gods. He obstinately insisted that he was wiser than anyone in his village regarding his actions.

In a bid to validate his desirability among young women, Mkulima resolved to acquire a second wife. It didn't take long before he forcibly brought in a modern girlfriend, reminiscent of Clementine in Okot's *Song of Lawino*. She could keep up with the pace of their outings, open beer bottles with ease, and was a stark contrast to his old-fashioned wife. His wife's tears and warnings fell on deaf ears, for Mkulima was already on a journey of self-destruction.

The new wife had become his career wife, the one he could take with him to draw his salary from the bank in the city. When the money entered his pocket, the two of them would spend their evenings in clubs until the stroke of midnight. On their way back home, they would ask for food that they had not provided for. "But we are Christians—you can't do this!" his first wife cried. "But I am the man; I can get married to as many wives as I want," he replied arrogantly. "Money is the devil," the village mumbled. "The richness itches in the fool man's pockets," people said.

Despite Mkulima's foolishness, his first wife continued to be loyal, as tradition had ingrained in her. She prayed harder, as the church had taught her, hoping that the dead tree could miraculously sprout again. She held onto the belief that things would eventually return to how they once were. "This is your temptation," the prayer fellows encouraged her. Yet nothing changed, and her prayers were never answered. In the end, she was forced to adapt and learn to navigate her new life in the marriage of wife-sisterhood.

With her humble disposition, the wife refused to surrender easily, determined to salvage her marriage. She had invested her life in building a family, and she wasn't going to let it crumble carelessly. However, each passing day only seemed to exacerbate the situation. Mkulima had transitioned from mental to physical abuse, an uncharted territory for his once gentle wife. It was becoming evident that money and love have problem sharing the same pot. That is why the marriages of the poor are destined to last.

People with nothing have each other but those with everything tend to lose each other in their hearts.

All efforts were futile, and the rightful wife had no choice but to flee the house to avoid becoming a statistic of domestic violence. The two suitors were left to revel in the spoils of their newfound union. Children, some still reliant on their parents, followed their mother. Consequently, the father of five was left to indulge in his youthfulness with his new paramour.

Things could not be better! The two would leave the house before sunrise and return home after midnight. Life was heavenly with no human distractions. Mkulima and his new wife were in heaven, although only immersed in a temporary anesthetic ecstasy of forgetfulness.

As their fondness ripened, Mkulima's work began to deteriorate. A year later, he received warnings about his performance. But before he could readjust his work ethics, he faced redundancy. Now he was a retired "handsome" with enough cash in his pockets. We all know how this goes.

Where else would his pension go if not to the bar? To show off his newfound wealth to his drinking mates that he was now richer than before. The "educated," as he bragged, would ask for "bring as many as we are." Beers would pour on his table, and people feasted. When he paid the bill, he never requested change or was too drunk to remember to ask for it. He was too intoxicated to know how much money he owed. People say his girlfriend, or rather his new wife, would make him drink to the point of speaking nonsensical English. She would then drag him home, and on the way, as one might expect, the "gold digger" would search his pockets to collect all the money she could find. This was the kind of man whose pockets were his servants.

Yet the retired veterinarian never learned his lesson. The ear of a dying man never perceives medicine. "This woman must have bewitched him," people murmured. "He is now putty in her hands," others added. And when he woke up in the morning after a hangover, he would wonder, "Honey, I thought I had kept a thousand shillings in my pocket!" "I don't know, we were all drunk last night, honey," she would tell him. "And what happened to the ones behind the shelves?" "There was money behind the shelves! I did not see them, honey! That's why you should let me keep the money— you get too drunk," the woman replied. Little by little, the pension he had received upon his retirement began to dissolve. The bank bag that held it behind his cupboard wall began to shrink. Smaller and smaller here it goes.

The legend goes, "do not desire a woman with big boobs if you have no money." Yet such adages are merely stereotypes. Let us instead focus on the old tale that "love is blind." This type of blindness causes lovers to utter sweet nothings, such as "I cannot sleep, for I dream of you," as if dreaming and reality are one and the same. As for Mkulima, he found himself in a rough speed to keep up with his new dreamy, stylish wife, except through lavish spending. Now, all of his money is gone, or to be more blunt, it was stolen by his conniving spouse. Yet he could not see it. Once his pockets were emptied, he resorted to selling his cows, one by one, until none remained. The land that he had worked so hard to obtain followed next, as he sold it piece by piece to keep up with his extravagant lifestyle.

As the familiar Swahili saying goes, *"kufa kufaana"*—one's death is another person's fortune. To the villagers, Mkulima's downfall was their fortune. Every morning, they eagerly listened to find out what the foolish man was auctioning that day. They whispered among themselves, "What is he selling today?" Those who had never owned a mattress were quick to snatch them up at rock-bottom prices. And when the mattress money ran out, Mkulima sold his beds to keep up with his wife's partying hobby.

But "love is blind," and Mkulima never learned. He continued to sell off his possessions, from couches to dinner tables, until he had nothing left. Foolishness, it seems, is a talent.

Mkulima's downfall came at the hands of a woman who drained him of his retirement savings. To him, she was nothing more than a pair of nibbling lips, but to her, he was a mindless "money tree" ripe for the picking. What man can think straight when trapped between the confines of a woman's thighs? Their allure has a power of stealing even the most sensible of men's common sense. The curve of a buttock is a weapon of mass destruction. Its throbs misplace men's virtues. What wisdom comes with an erect penis? Is a man's scrotum not a substitute for their brain? That was it. What had brought Adam down the garden was the same fruit that was bringing Mkulima down.

With each passing day, Mkulima descended further into the abyss of his lover's avarice. The once sturdy doors of his abode were the first to fall prey to his desperate hands, followed shortly by the windows, leaving his abode an open wound to the world outside. All the while, he chased after the fleeting promise of love, unaware that his paramour cared only for his shallow pockets. As his material possessions dwindled, his motorcycle became the next target of their rapacious desires. Reduced to a pedestrian, they stumbled from the bar in a haze of intoxication and misery. And when there was scarcely anything left to sell, Mkulima resorted to tearing the iron sheets from his own roof in a futile attempt to satisfy his lover's insatiable cravings. The woman, her mission accomplished, departed without a word, taking with her every last scrap of change she could find in his meager hiding places.

She was now nowhere to be found. Who looked after her anyway? In a period of two or three years, the village witnessed the most glorified man in the area stripping himself naked. And when he was too exposed to be the guest of nobody, he, with no shame, moved back to his elderly mother's half-fallen muddy hut that he never attempted to modify. And when the rain fell that year, his abandoned roofless house became indistinguishable from an anthill. Unable to make sense of himself, the man had a mental breakdown. Before we knew it, he had lost touch with himself.

"His wealth was tied to his first wife," people murmured. Mkulima was now a vagrant, stumbling through the village with nothing but his British accent. "Boys, we better monitor our penis," young men joked to themselves. But to him, he was "the deaf ear that had never heard of medicine." The penis that once gave him manhood was the enemy to blame. "The man's poo is very odorous, dad!" I quipped to my father years later as we revisited his downfall. My father bellowed with mirth: "for this I concur, it stinks to high heaven!" My dad then added in Kirimi, *munyokhoja ugikhananteya,* meaning "but every pisser should shake off his own shit."

IX

-

And She is a Woman

—

WOMANNESS, IN MANY CULTURES in Tanzania, is intricately intertwined with the destiny of a man. This is why a man like Mkulima could not only determine the course of a woman's life but also, in the blink of an eye, render her future invisible. This harsh reality can be particularly daunting for women striving to effect positive change in their communities.

Having spent a year in Gumanga, I pursued my passion for music at Tumaini University. Upon completing my studies, I relocated to the city center of Singida to be with my wife, Deborah, who was then employed at the diocese office.

Deborah and I are from different ethnic groups in the Singida region. She is from the Wanyiramba tribe, and I am from the Arimi tribe. Although our cultures, traditions, and languages vary slightly, Tanzania, I must say, has dealt well with cultural tensions, and intermarriages are increasingly common.

For example, both Igengu and Gumanga, where I previously worked, were located in the Wanyiramba area. I therefore served primarily among the Wanyiramba people. However, Singida municipality, where Deborah worked, is primarily Arimi.

Deborah was appointed as the director of women for the entire diocese, a position in which she was responsible for developing programs to empower women and advocate for gender equality, not only for Christian women but also for children. However, gender equality issues are sensitive in Tanzania's patriarchal social and cultural structure, requiring a delicate approach.

The Singida region is known for having one of the highest rates of female genital mutilation (FGM) in the country. Deborah became passionate about FGM issues after her appointment. She acted as a bridge between the larger church and local communities in the central region of Tanzania, not acting alone but with the support of her colleagues.

Not all cultural groups in Tanzania practice female genital mutilation. Wanyiramba people, for example, where Deborah belongs to, did not practice it. It is also worth mentioning that FGM is illegal in Tanzania, but the practice is rooted deep in cultures where people practice it in secret. In cultures who practice it, one must be careful of challenging it, particularly if considered a cultural outsider. That was how I felt about my wife: "she must be careful."

One of the ways in which gender roles and discrimination are perpetuated is through social hierarchies. For instance, most Tanzanian societies are organized along patrilineal lines. In this system, generations descend through the man's lineage, with the father being the head of the clan. Moreover, clans are named after men. I will explain as an example, how this social structure is vividly illustrated in the Arimi people's homestead organization. The word "home" in our language, *ito*, denotes not only a house but also a sequence of houses divided into two main groups: women's houses (*nyumba akhema*) and men's houses (*idemu*).

Nyumba akhema is open to all women and girls living in the homestead, female neighbors, and female visitors. Conversely, the *idemu* is exclusively for men. This gendered arrangement symbolizes the "identity, power, hierarchy, femininity, and masculinity" that some scholars have attributed to social structures. From an early age, boys are groomed and prepared for the *ito* system. They undergo initiation rites of passage (*ngovi*), where they are instilled with *mahumo*, heavy teachings on the secrets of life, in readiness to start their own households (marriage). During these teachings, boys are indoctrinated to adopt a superior attitude towards girls, including their mothers. In contrast, girls are trained to be submissive to men. These purposeful sociological gender distinctions are intended to equip both genders with the necessary skills and roles to operate effectively in their social-cultural groups. Yet, they reflect the cruel nature of power dynamics, gender relations, and hierarchies.

Even in modern-day Tanzania, many families and cultures remain opposed to the notion of empowering women. The idea of enrolling a female child in school is still viewed as a waste of resources for some. This perspective stems from the belief that a girl's role is to remain at home and eventually get married. Moreover, only a few educated men are willing to marry an educated woman, as they perceive her as a threat to their masculinity.

In marriages, a woman is viewed as mere chattel, a possession of her husband. She is commodified and brought to the man to serve as a means of productivity. Men feel entitled to exercise dominion over their wives, even if that entails resorting to physical violence. As I previously alluded to, only men are the active agents in the process of "marrying," while women are merely passive recipients of the marital union. They are "married." Indeed, it is a social convention that dictates that no woman, regardless of how modern or progressive she may be, is expected to take the initiative to express her feelings of love or desire for marriage to a man. The entire ritual of "marrying" and "loving" is structured such that the man is the active "doer," while the woman is relegated to the passive role of receiver.

This means that in marriage, a woman not only becomes the property of her husband, but she also ceases to exist without him. Consequently, a woman's womanhood is contingent upon her marital status and her association with her husband. It is fair to assert that the womanhood of an unmarried woman is regarded as inferior to that of a married woman. This perception exerts immense pressure on unmarried, married, and divorced women alike to subsume their own identities to that of their husbands, even in the context of a toxic relationship. Regrettably, this is the painful reality.

In the event that a husband dies, some wives, particularly those who are younger, may return to their parents. However, this only occurs if the woman intends to remarry, as leaving her children and everything else to her late husband's family is considered a necessary sacrifice. In most Tanzanian cultures, a married woman is inextricably linked not only to her husband but also to his family and clan. People would say, "she is our wife," theoretically, but in some cultures, "our" can also be interpreted in a physical sense. The clan or family would cling to "their wife" for as long as she has children of their son and agrees to remain. For some women, they may even be inherited by one of their brothers-in-law, as dictated by protocol. They become a part of that particular tradition or clan, and only a handful of them have the autonomy to leave that *boma* and remarry elsewhere. And when that happens, the woman must be forced to leave everything she earned with her husband behind, regardless of the presence of the law against that.

At the bus station, Deborah was on her way to lead a seminar on women and children's rights. As she waited for the bus, she noticed a woman named Bula, who had been sitting quietly and weeping. Deborah approached her, struck by her distress.

Bula, a stranger to Deborah, confided that she had lost her husband and had nowhere to go. Her brothers-in-law had taken everything from her, including eighteen acres of land, a modern house, a tractor, and a motorbike. Bula's only option was to board a bus and travel aimlessly because she had nowhere to turn.

Deborah was taken aback by Bula's plight, and although she wasn't a lawyer, she knew how to find one. With a vast network of legal experts and organizations, Deborah swiftly arranged an appointment for Bula with a lawyer and directed her to a prominent human rights organization. Bula's case was in the right hands and Deborah had forgotten about this encounter.

Time passed, and one day, Deborah received a phone call from an unfamiliar number. The voice on the other end of the line was that of a woman, and she was weeping uncontrollably. Though she did not introduce herself, she expressed profound gratitude to Deborah, saying, "I don't know if you remember me, but I want you to know how much I appreciate what you did for me. You gave me my life back."

Deborah, who had met countless women in her work, was momentarily confused and asked the woman for her name. "My name is Bula," the woman replied, "I'm the woman you helped at the bus stop."

Deborah was overjoyed to hear from Bula, whom she had not heard from in nearly a year. They had not exchanged contact information, yet Bula had managed to track down Deborah's number. She informed Deborah that she had won her case, and her properties had been rightfully returned to her.

Deborah was left speechless, humbled by the power of chance encounters and the impact of her work. She reflected on how the universe had conspired to bring them together, and how Bula's call had renewed her sense of purpose.

****

Deborah had done so much at this point; the work that was not only inspiring but also a testament to the power of advocacy for gender equality. As we will see later, her work was a demonstration that one person, armed with compassion and determination, could make a substantial difference in the lives of others. Bula's case was only a small symbol of hope and resilience against gender injustices, and Deborah's unwavering commitment to justice serves as an exemplar to all those who seek to make a positive impact on the world.

Cultural structures and situations in Tanzania have prevalently empowered men like Mkulima and in-laws to throw women under the bus. These practices are customary despite the fact that laws against these very atrocities are enshrined in the Tanzanian constitution. But having laws and enforcing them, or rather the awareness of those laws, are separate things.

I will come back to Deborah's work, but I must close my Gumanga page first. On a regular basis, two legal systems coexist in Tanzania: the traditional system and the judiciary system. This duality creates a loophole that grants power to people like Mkulima to eject their legal wives without any compensation. One might even kill their wives, like what we have seen with Nikota, and yet the matter is covered up or resolved traditionally. Often, when it comes to inequalities, injustices, and domestic abuse, women are the problem and the victims. And most of these women have no basic knowledge of laws that protect them. After two years of marriage, Deborah, my wife, would be the one to take on this task—to educate them about their legal rights.

As I mentioned earlier, communities in Tanzania operate between legal and cultural forces. There is a thin line between what should be handled legally versus traditionally. In many cases, cultural repressive practices win. Thus, even for those marriages that are Christian, they are often influenced by traditional/cultural ways of life. This was still the case in Gumanga.

The marriage arrangement, even one held in church like Joyce's, involves many moving parts. While the church might set a wedding day, families continue to clear up traditional requirements that might slow down the process. But sometimes things to determine are not easy. For example, a father from either side might delay a marriage for any reason. From the woman's side, it usually something about the unpaid dowry. This happened to me while still in Gumanga.

I had put on my pastoral robe to bless the marriage when the church elder approached me, asking that I must postpone that service. "Postpone!

What does that mean?" I asked him. At this time, the groom and I had been waiting for the bride to appear for almost an hour. We had stood at the pulpit waiting, but it seemed something was going on outside. I took off my robe and walked to the crowded elders on a church's corner.

"What's wrong?" I asked them.

"This marriage is not legitimate, Pastor."

"Legitimate . . . how? What do you mean not legitimate?"

"The groom owes me a goat," the father of the bride said. "He needs to pay for the last dowry," he explained.

"A goat?" I probed.

"Yes."

"Why did you wait until today?"

"Well, he was going to pay. He—he said he would pay."

"And . . ." I prompted him to finish his response, with obvious anger on my face.

"He—he did not pay," he answered with the fatherly tone of a girl's ownership.

"And I say, he will pay later," I let my voice trail as I walked away furiously. "Bring the bride into the sanctuary; otherwise, I will sue you," I commanded the worship leaders who had been negotiating with the father all this time. People looked at me hesitantly as if questioning my authority. "Did you hear what I just said? Bring in the bride in the sanctuary." I commanded angrily while entering the church door.

As I approached the pulpit, I couldn't help but think to myself, "A goat? How selfish!" However, before I delve into the occurrence that led me there, allow me to provide some context.

Upon my arrival in Gumanga, I was faced with a daunting task—helping a man and a woman who had been living together for over fifteen years without an official marriage. The man, initially a Muslim, had converted to Christianity to be with his wife. Together, they had children and loved each other deeply. However, despite their commitment, they had never made their union official due to a multitude of barriers. When I asked what those barriers were, the man revealed that he had grown up without parents and suffered from physical disabilities, yet he still managed to provide for his family. They both agreed to make their marriage official, but their main concern was the expense of a wedding ceremony.

During a lengthy conversation, I explained to them that a wedding ceremony was not a requirement for a legal marriage. "All you need is your consented love and a pastor," I reassured them. The couple was overjoyed as if this news had been kept hidden from them for all those years. Without hesitation, preparations began.

I informed my church elders and several individuals who offered to help with expenses and preparations. One week before the wedding, I rode my bicycle uphill to meet the couple for final touches. As they welcomed me in, I sensed a somber atmosphere, unlike anything I had seen on their faces before. I knew immediately that something was wrong, but I hoped that they had not changed their minds.

"Tell me," I said. "Something is wrong. What is it?" The man looked at me as if to ask how I knew, then replied, "Pastor, to be honest, we are sorry to tell you, but our marriage is cancelled. We don't know what to tell you," he said vaguely.

"Cancelled? Who cancelled it? Who else would cancel your wedding except for yourselves?" I asked indignantly as I stepped closer to them. "My parents," the woman replied, likely on behalf of her husband. "They asked my husband to pay the full dowry before allowing us to proceed with the marriage." At this time, I felt as if I wanted to punch someone in the face.

"What dowry, and why now?" I retorted. "Are they insane? You've lived together for fifteen years!" I exclaimed furiously as if they were the cause.

"Yes, we have children, Pastor," the woman replied helplessly.

"So what's the point? Will they separate you now?"

"No, they just object to the marriage until we pay the dowry," she explained.

"Object! Okay, listen. Are you ready for your wedding or not?" I asked fiercely.

"Yes, we . . . we are, but . . ." a man stuttered as if not sure that could be the option.

"That's enough for me!" I interrupted. "I'm the only person with a legal certification to unite or cancel a wedding in this congregation. Next Sunday, you will be married as planned. Whatever your parents decide to do afterward will be up to me. Okay?" And with that, I left their house.

While family loyalty, cultural norms, and traditions are all admirable things, they can become burdensome when abused. Furthermore, some norms are pointless even for those who follow them. The couple had lived together for years without issue, yet when they decided to formalize their union, their parents found a way to mask their greed behind cultural norms.

This situation was particularly upsetting because the man was disabled and poor. Waiting for him to pay the bride price fully and cover his marriage are what have led them staying unmarried. Yet, the woman had fallen in love with him unconditionally and the two made great parents. Without an official marriage certificate, however, any issues that arose could potentially result in a loss of rights. But how did we get here? Was African culture always gendered?

****

Circumstances such as these are a stark reminder that those who have the power to help also possess the power to hurt. In Singida, such was the case when I received a distressing call from a woman, which my colleague Majengo and I answered. The caller, with a sense of urgency, implored us to visit her home immediately. Her message was brief and ominous: "Pastor, please come to our house without delay."

Unsure of what lay ahead, we set off, armed only with the pastor's most precious tool, the Bible. As we arrived at the house, the woman was waiting at the door, anxiety etched across her face. Without exchanging any pleasantries, she informed us that her husband was dying. He had been diagnosed with HIV-AIDS several years earlier, and now his final moments were upon him.

The man had slipped into a coma a week before but miraculously bounced back, only to be discharged from the hospital and sent back home. However, his health rapidly deteriorated, and now he lay at death's door. As we spoke outside the house, a car was called to take him to the hospital one last time. Neighbors had gathered to assist with moving him to the vehicle. "This is his final journey. He won't make it back," the woman said in a choked voice.

With a heavy heart, the woman ushered us into the house to meet her husband for the first time. She disappeared into the room, leaving us waiting in the somber living room. As she emerged, supporting her husband, it was evident that every step was a struggle. He was in obvious discomfort, attempting to lower his back as we watched him intently from his toes to his head. Witnessing the ravages of the virus on a human being was an excruciating experience. AIDS is a merciless disease that strips away everything that defines a person. The man, once notable and esteemed, had been consumed by an invisible bug, leaving nothing but a fleeting glance of remorseful eyes. It was as the Swahili proverb says: "if you are not dead, you are not formed," meaning a person is one of the walking dead. A man could now fit in the palm of one's hand.

I had never encountered a person in such a dire condition, and I found myself helplessly echoing the rhythms of his breath as he struggled to lift his eyelashes to acknowledge our presence. His attempts to speak were feeble, with his words stumbling and faltering along with his labored breaths. "What is he trying to say?" I asked his wife, my voice heavy with sorrow. As if acting as a translator, she replied, "He is grateful that you could come." My heart sank with empathy, and I replied, "Oh dear . . . we are grateful to see you."

The room was filled with a heavy silence, only broken by the man's expensive breaths. My words seemed to have abandoned me, leaving me struggling to keep the conversation going. Majengo, noticing my paralysis, gave me a look that signaled for me to hurry. "What . . . what would you like us to do?" I asked hesitantly, not expecting much in response. My impression was that they wanted us to say a short prayer before they left for the hospital. In response to my question, the man mumbled incoherently. I leaned towards him, trying to capture his beaten-up words. "What did he say?" I asked his wife again. She explained with a strained smile, "I think he wants to tell you the whole story."

"Can we please clear the room?" I found myself yelling to some uninvited neighbors who had already gathered into a small crowd. "Clear the room, please!" I shouted again. "I only need two church elders here—others, please wait outside," I commanded to secure some fresh air.

In a few minutes, the woman told their story, and it was preoccupying. After the man discovered he had HIV, not wanting to harm his wife, he decided to inform her. "He confided in me, 'I decided not to have a sexual relationship with you. That way, when I die, you will be able to take care of our children and properties,'" the woman testified on his behalf. "Have you been tested?" Majengo asked. "Yes, I have tested—more than once, and I am fine. We haven't had a sexual encounter for a long time. He used to travel a lot for his business," she added. "Wow!" I exclaimed uncontrollably. To this day, I still cannot make sense of how that miracle happened.

I couldn't help but feel a sense of awe and wonder at this revelation. The couple had been blessed with beautiful children, a house in the city, and money. He was a wealthy man, most of which he spent on other women. However, and this is the crucial point, his marriage with his present woman of many years was not official. Now he was approaching his last moments, and the couple had pondered, "what if he dies?" "He had wanted us to get married—he thought it would be better if we come to church for our official marriage, but now in this condition, we don't know what is next," a woman wailed.

I turned to the man, still conscious but barely so. "What do you want us to do?" I asked, my voice mixed with sadness. He raised his head slightly, licking his cracked dry lips. "We want to . . ." he trailed off, his voice barely audible. "What is he saying?" I asked the woman, my heart aching. "He wants us to get married," she replied, her voice barely above a whisper.

I looked over at Majengo, hoping for some guidance, but this time his eyes were downcast to repel my gaze. I turned back to the Bible in my hands, searching for any relevant text to guide me. The only verse that I could think of was the conversation between Philip and the Ethiopian eunuch: "We have water and the Scripture; what forbids us from baptism?" I looked at the woman again, her eyes filled with desperation. "All right. Majengo, what do you think? I suppose we have no objections to this marriage, do we?" I said softly.

Majengo's response was a dry gaze, one that conveyed the urgency of the situation. I took the couple's hands in mine and blessed them, skipping the whole lengthy liturgy. "What God has joined together, let no one separate," I declared without further questioning what that even meant for them.

The whole process, from our arrival to the blessing, took less than fifteen minutes. The man struggled to say "thank you" and was carried to the car for his "last journey." The following day, the woman came to collect their wedding certificate from my office, explaining that her husband was unresponsive. As expected, he passed away the next morning.

The man's body was transported to his village, far from Singida, for a burial. About two weeks later, the woman and her children returned, and Majengo and I went to pay our respects to her late husband. As we sat down, the woman spoke with a sorrowful voice, "You are God's messengers. My life would have been over," she continued, her voice trembling with emotion. "And you should not be thanking us; thank your bravery," Majengo comforted her.

This couple had a compelling reason to be officially married. After the woman's husband was laid to rest, her brothers-in-law came to her, seeking to take all of their shared property, including a bank account. As the woman recounted, "They knew I was not legally married to their brother, and so they wanted to kick me out of my house. After they found out that we were officially married, they went back home very angry. They don't want to speak to me anymore, but I don't care. I just thank God for you, the church, my family, and I would have had nowhere to go," she wept between joy and loss.

"God is so mysterious," Majengo would later reflect. "Indeed he is," I replied, lost in thought. I had not anticipated officiating a wedding, but I was glad we had done the right thing. As we left the house that afternoon, Majengo commented in a contemplative voice, "If you can help, you can also hurt. We could have hurt this woman, but we did the right thing."

Years later, as I reflect on that moment, I can't help but wonder about the depth of this love and the sorrow that the woman must have felt as she said goodbye to her husband. The heaviness of his confession must have been crushing, yet she chose to embrace the fleeting moments they had left together and make them count. Would it have been the same if the problem was reversed? That I cannot say. But her unwavering love stood as a story of itself; the attestation to immense sacrifices women make and the remarkable resilience of their human spirit.

X

-

The Uphill Battle for Change

—

I BEGAN TO WRITE this book to remember some of my encounters with women's experiences in Tanzanian cultures. However, I am not suggesting that anybody is born with the culture. For me, culture is an accident of history and evolution, a reflection of our inherent failures to achieve uniformity. We are all cultureless before we are born. We come to be introduced to it somewhere in our mother's wombs. In the womb we begin grasping for food, music, dance, and being oriented in landscapes and patterns. The moment we attempt our first breath on earth, we are partially baptized as cultural. Soon our parents' culture becomes ours. Soon the culture becomes us, the mold through which all of us must be transformed to become. And all of a sudden, it begins to manifest itself in and outside ourselves in many forms.

I often contemplate how culture takes root within an individual. This question brings to mind a particular year when, during one of my holidays, I visited a family in my local area. Upon my arrival, a three-year-old boy who was playing outside approached me, his curious eyes fixed on my rented bicycle. In what I found to be an amusing inquiry, he posed the question, "Is your bicycle a boy or a girl?"

Momentarily flustered, I inquired as to what he meant by his question. Without hesitation, he repeated the query, leaving me speechless. It seemed preposterous to me that a young child would assign a gender to an inanimate object, especially one as clearly devoid of gender as a bicycle.

This interaction made me consider how children learn to identify objects in the world around them and how this process is influenced by their culture. The way that we understand and perceive objects is closely linked to our cultural background, and the notion of gender is a prime example of this. It happens everywhere and can take many forms, but I cannot speak for the world. In our Tanzanian cultures, gender is a pervasive and deeply ingrained concept, shaping not only how we perceive ourselves and others but also how we interpret the world.

I attempted to explain to a young boy the gender neutrality of a bicycle but struggled to provide a convincing answer. I gathered my thoughts and sought to articulate a more thoughtful response. I explained that objects like bicycles, stones, and cars do not have a gender, as they are not living beings. However, the boy remained unconvinced and pressed me further, asking "Why?" repeatedly.

"Why!—why what? Because things like a bicycle do not have a particular sex—they are 'things,' not people; they cannot be a boy or a girl," I explained in a childish way. "But why?" he insisted.

"Because a bicycle does not have 'boy' or girl'—See! It is not a person."

"I know, but why?" he insisted.

"Why? Because things are not like a cow or a goat—look! This is made of metals—you see? Look at that chicken—it can be a girl but not this metal—look!"

"But why it is not a girl or a boy?" he insisted.

Well, a few minutes have passed, and I could not answer the simplest "why" question from a three years old kid. To end this non-ending conversation with the boy who was already disappointed by my irrational answers, I surrendered my stupidity. Realizing my failures, I turned unto him for a help. I finally said "I don't know 'why.' Do you know why?"

He then said, "Yes, I know." "So, which do you think the bicycle is—a boy or a girl?" To my question, this little dirty villager, answered very confidently, "I think your bicycle is a boy." "Oh! Okay—and why do you think it is a boy?" I asked him. "I just think it is a boy," he said while running away to join his friends who were already playing on the other side of the yard. "Right then, let's say it is a boy" I concluded to myself.

Culture shapes the way we think and perceive the world around us. I witnessed this firsthand in a three-year-old boy, who already displayed an understanding of gender roles and stereotypes. Children learn how to identify objects and people based on the cultural constructions of their society. Since gender roles are cultural, they cannot be fixed or biologically informed but rather are cultural constructs that vary across societies. We are not born with a specific roles, norms, values, or expectations, but we become assigned through elements of our social-cultural upbringing such as practices, beliefs, and attitudes.

While biology may determine our sex, it is culture that shapes our gender identity and how we express it. Our culture creates expectations for how men and women should behave, think, and interact with one another. These expectations are often deeply ingrained and unconscious, making it difficult to recognize them as cultural constructions.

Over time, our culture shapes us as individuals and as a society, and we internalize its norms and values. Our humanness becomes intertwined with cultural norms to the point where we may not even be aware of their influence on us. The interplay between our culture and our humanity is so intertwined that it becomes difficult to distinguish one from the other. We must therefore, be mindful of the cultural constructions that shape our thinking and strive to challenge them in order to create a more equitable and just society.

The challenge lies in the fact that culture is like a constantly flowing river that carries everything along with it, both living and dead. The fish in the river, for example, view it as their entire world and are unable to see beyond its boundaries. While the river can change the direction of the fish, the fish are unable to alter the course of the river, particularly when acting in accordance with its principles.

Furthermore, for the fish, every direction may seem the same, as what matters most to them is the water, not its direction. Without standing on the riverbank, the fish are unable to perceive or question why the river flows in a particular direction or why it behaves as it does.

However, standing on the edge of the river also puts the fish in peril, risking their very lives. It is only through that death that rebirth and trans-formation can occur. And since the river carries all creatures along its path, what consumed the mother is likely to consume the daughter unless out-side forces intervene. Like the river, culture has no issue maintaining its direction unless redirected by external influences.

Changing a culture is akin to changing a person, and it is nearly im-possible to achieve. To change a person's culture is to effectively "kill" that person within their cultural identity. Even with the promise of resurrection, as in Christian theology, death is still a terrifying prospect. Thus, changing culture is almost as challenging as changing the individual who embodies that culture, as culture and people are intrinsically intertwined.

****

"I will inquire of my father; I will inquire of my mother. Who is the creator, the one responsible for our existence? What entity fashioned this unique and distinct creation, intended for all of humanity to adhere to? What an awe-inspiring creation it is!" As Nyasema's song reverberates, these words are but an excerpt from the *isunga* song, a prevalent genre during initiation ceremonies to prepare both boys and girls to become men and women.

****

At Kititimo parsonage, six locally forged blades lay on our living room table. I'm referring to recycled tin blades, handcrafted by local artisans. They had been sharpened along one edge and had their ends bent like a fishhook. Deborah and I examined them one by one. Each was tied with a dirty strip made from an old rag, which was used to hang these tools from the ceiling after they had torn open the girls' foreskins. They have turned black from a smoke circulating from the kitchen where they hung. That smoke was meant to "sterilize" them for their next use.

The surgical blades before us were a haunting sight, stained with a murky blend of girls' blood and tears and reeking of their ruthless purpose. These instruments of torture had inflicted untold agony, extinguished countless joys, and shattered countless dreams. Ritual after ritual, *rika* to *rika*. Memories after memories carved in their existence. What stories do they tell? What bravery do they recall? Of those on which my mother would comment, "I had to become a woman." Now, gazing upon these blades, I knew that it was time for that story to be told.

As I contemplated these traditional surgical blades in silence, my wife interrupted my thoughts. "What do you think?" she asked, looking at me after staring intently at the objects. "I don't know what to think," I replied. "Six practitioners have turned in these blades to me. Can you imagine? You can't believe the stories they've told me." Her eyes filled with sadness as she continued, "I didn't know such violence existed among my fellow women. I am so sad and scared."

Each day was different. My wife's calendar started to fill up with scribbles. She grouped people according to sex, age, status, education, beliefs, and all possible categories. On one of her campaigns, she met with forty local government officials, thirty-eight of whom were men and two women. She taught them all about the effects of genital mutilation. "I'm happy to report the following," she said. "They were all astonished to hear about these big issues. They didn't expect them, especially from a woman. I know some of them were annoyed."

Through her tireless efforts, my wife was able to convince many leaders to disclose how they go about the practice. Some men admitted perpetuating the practice due to ignorance, while others acknowledged the lack of knowledge about basic human rights. Female participants opened up about their irresponsible behavior towards their families, particularly their daughters. Some men expressed shock at discovering their wives' lack of enjoyment in their marriages, but were unsure how to broach the subject given the taboo nature of sexual education in their communities.

Deborah was overcome with a sense of sadness and despair when she discovered that these midwives had never received any formal training on the harmful effects of FGM. It was as if their lack of education had condemned countless innocent girls to a lifetime of pain and suffering. The task of changing these deeply ingrained beliefs proved to be an insurmountable challenge, but they remained committed to their cause.

As they presented the information, they were met with resistance and skepticism from the midwives. Many of the local leaders were too timid to discuss the matter, and the midwives' illiteracy compounded the challenge. Even those who had stopped performing FGM did so out of fear of retribution from the authorities, rather than an understanding of the immense harm it causes.

They poured their hearts and souls into their mission, but progress was slow and arduous. It was evident that change would not happen overnight. They needed to develop a program tailored to age-set groups and ensure follow-up to verify that those who received the seminars implemented the knowledge.

As I watched my wife pore over her notes, I marveled at her dedication to her cause. Her desk was strewn with books, articles, and colorful marker pens, while her computer was filled with detailed reports and program notes. It seemed as though our bedroom had become a storage room, with papers and notes spilling out of every nook and cranny. But despite the chaos, my wife remained focused, determined to prepare for her upcoming meeting with local midwives, traditional surgeons, local officials, and respected elders.

As she reviewed her budget, my wife turned to me and asked for assistance in selecting women to attend a national workshop. I was eager to help, but in truth, I was simply in awe of her tireless efforts. She was more than a witch doctor—she was a theologian, a scientist, and a psychologist, all rolled into one.

Curious about her process, I asked, "What do you do after you meet with them? How do you even begin?" "Do you think it's easy?" she replied, smiling wryly. "I start slowly, by telling their stories and singing their songs. As I sing, they start to dance, and I join in. They are always surprised by my skills, and it helps to break down the barriers between us. After they are motivated, they forget who they are, and sometimes they even laugh at my poor pronunciation of their language. But this is what makes them listen, and it's what helps them to trust me."

I couldn't help but be impressed by her approach. It wasn't easy, what she was doing, and I knew that firsthand. When my wife first started this program with other people, she was met with skepticism and even hostility. No one wanted to listen to her, to take her seriously. How could she, an outsider, understand their experiences? How could she hope to argue with those who were born into traditions that included genital mutilation? And how could she convince them that the cutting of the clitoris took away their sexual pleasure, when many of these women had been raised to believe that sex was something to be feared and avoided?

It was a daunting task, but my wife never gave up. She learned to approach these communities with patience and compassion, sharing their stories and listening to their experiences. And slowly but surely, she began to make progress.

Over time, my wife's work began to bear fruit. She held seminars and workshops around Singida and beyond, and as she did, and as she did, she watched as local leaders began to take notice. They began to facilitate their own seminars, spreading the word to others in their communities. And while there were still obstacles to overcome —the entrenched beliefs and customs that upheld these practices—my wife remained steadfast in her commitment to bringing about change.

IX

-

Forbidden Dreams to Pursuing Womanhood

—

"I THINK MAMA (NYASEMA) can help me with this," my wife told me one evening as we sat in our living room. "Her experience with women and culture is a potential learning tool if I could take her for some more training. She will be able to teach about the effects of genital mutilation than me." "I think that is a good idea," I agreed. That evening, Deborah phoned my mother.

Nyasema's story begins with her role as a midwife. While some may question her professional qualifications, she has consistently demonstrated her ability to safely deliver babies, earning the reputation of having "pure hands." She has aided countless newborns, including her own children—seven in total, with the eighth lost too soon to be remembered. As she put it, "I have suctioned the noses of many babies and cut many umbilical cords."

Her own mother was also a midwife. "I believe I inherited her skills, even though I didn't practice midwifery until I delivered your older sister," Nyasema would tell me. The rest of her story goes as follows:

"I was at the clinic for my first pregnancy, surrounded by other pregnant women—all of us exhausted, our protruding bellies weighing us down (she chuckles). While waiting for a nurse to call our names, one of the women began to experience labor pains."

"I was the only one light enough to run and fetch help, so I dashed off to find a nurse. Unfortunately, the nurse on duty was just an inexperienced

107

intern (she said disdainfully). I informed her that the woman was in labor, but she didn't listen to me, instead looking at me as if I were a puppet, pursing her lips and carrying on with her other duties!" Nyasema recounted, revealing her irritation.

"I insisted: 'There's a woman out there about to give birth in the corridor!' But she ignored me and began berating me, 'Pregnant women are so troublesome! You've only just arrived—can't you be patient? We have work to do here,'" Nyasema imitated the nurse. "I was ready to slap her, but . . ." she said with emphasis, trailing off as we all laughed.

"What did you do then?" I asked.

"I went back and told the other women to wait," she quipped. "Wait?" we all exclaimed. "Hahaha, can you imagine? How do you ask a woman who's about to give birth to wait?" Nyasema quipped.

"When I arrived, the baby was practically at *the door*. The woman was sobbing uncontrollably, and the other women were at a loss for what to do. I looked at the new mother and thought, 'You know what? I can do this.' I instructed the other women to create a makeshift privacy screen using our Khangas, as we were still in the reception area. I locked eyes with the mother and gave her a serious look. 'Listen to me,' I said. 'If it was fated for you to die today, even a nurse wouldn't be able to save you. But listen to me carefully. Take a deep breath and push. Push with all your might!'"

"The woman pushed—and pushed with incredible determination, pushing through the pain and exhaustion until the baby finally emerged, a robust and healthy baby boy. The sound of his first cries echoed through the room, and the nurse hurried over, hastily attempting to don gloves before reaching for the newborn. But it was too late—my mother had already cradled him in her arms. The nurse looked abashed, met with the scowls and angry shouts of the other women present. It's a wonder how some people manage to get such important jobs," my mother added, her face twisted in disgust.

"Mama, really?" I asked, incredulous.

My mom laughed. That was her first baby delivery. Since then, Nyasema became known throughout all the nearby villages. Even though Mtinko has a moderate hospital these days, pregnant women prefer to be assisted by Nyasema instead of going to the hospital. And she never charged them; she did it all for free. Only a few mothers would honor her with small gifts like a bowl of corn flour or a chicken. Some even honored her by naming their babies after her. But her motivation has never been about material things. She says her joy is to welcome new humans into the world

When I was still residing with my parents, on occasion, my mother would be awakened from her slumber by a knock on the door from someone whose spouse was giving birth. At times, she would abandon a pot of lunch simmering on the cooking rocks to assist a neighbor in labor. One day, she left the house to fetch water, leaving behind a pot of dinner on the stove. The pot boiled until all the water evaporated, and she was still not back. Nobody was home that day except for my father and me, and as you may know, Arimi men are not proficient in cooking. Thus, we waited and waited without any sight of her. And then, all of a sudden, she appeared, but she was not carrying a bucket of water. Instead, she was carrying a newborn, wrapped in a *khanga*. As she approached the house, singing as she usually does, we all marveled, "Where did she acquire this baby?"

Despite my father's anger at my mother's tardiness, when mom approached the doorpost, a joyful bend of her neck, casting her gaze upon us, changed the mood. She then playfully quipped, "Look what I found for you at the well—a baby!" The wittiness of her remark drew laughter from all of us. I couldn't help but ask her in astonishment, "Whose baby is this?" Before she could answer, a new mother was ushered in, supported by her mother-in-law and other women who had accompanied her.

It turned out that while my mother was on her way to fetch water, she noticed a pregnant woman being transported on a bicycle. Suddenly, the woman could no longer bear the discomfort and requested to be taken off the bike due to contractions. Her baby was on the way. The women who accompanied the pregnant woman had no choice but to leave things to chance, as they had learned to do. In a place where even seeing a car was a rare occurrence, the bicycle served as an ambulance, pushed uphill by men. Despite their efforts, they were unable to transport the woman to the nearest Mtinko hospital, which was still some miles away. However, my mother, who was not far away, saw the scene and knew what needed to be done. She has an instinct for when it is time. It was clear that the woman was about to give birth on the side of the road.

When my mother was young, she had a fierce desire to attend school. "If I had studied, I would have achieved great things," she would often say. She often reflected on her childhood, recalling how her parents resisted the idea of her going to school. Like many others, my mom's parents viewed education with suspicion and feared that sending their children to school would mean losing them to the white man's ways. They believed that her place was at home, helping with household chores and eventually getting married.

Despite the cultural norm of the time, which dictated that girls were expected to remain at home and work on household duties, my mother never stopped longing for the opportunity to learn. However, the schools available to children during those days were few and far between, mostly run by white missionaries.

To fill in these schools, white fathers would visit families in the area to negotiate with parents to let their children attend. During these visits, many parents hid. They believed that schools would rob them of their culture and turn them into "Europeans." The white fathers would try to reassure parents that their children would return home and not lose touch with their roots. Despite the government's insistence that children attend school, many parents still send their children away when the teachers arrived. "Who would want their child to be taken away by white missionaries?" my mother recalls. "If you let them go, they won't come back. They will no longer belong to you," she adds, referring to how her parents thought of education at the time. Despite the many obstacles, my mother's desire for education never waned.

"Teachers came to my parents' home to ask for my attendance in school many times," my mother recounted. But my father staunchly resisted the teachers' request. Her father cherished his daughter and felt that allowing her to attend school put her in danger of being taken away. My mother and her brother were expected to help with house chores and tend to the cattle, so schooling was forbidden.

During the summer, Nyasema would join other girls in the village to trek miles to the forest to collect firewood. "We spent the entire afternoon gathering firewood and returned home late in the evening. Some of the girls would tire out and abandon their bundles along the way but not me. I was a master at collecting firewood, and my parents appreciated my hard work. In the village, my collection was unrivaled—I arranged the sticks aesthetically, sizing and placing them meticulously one by one. I was very particular and detail-oriented, despite being smaller than my agemates. I could carry two bundles of firewood, the larger one on top of my head and the smaller one in my hands. Most of my friends were sluggish and wouldn't even cut the woods to the same lengths."

The seemingly simple act of collecting firewood carried significant weight in her community. Her skill in the art of bundling firewood was admired by all who visited her parents' home, with carefully stacked and bound bundles that served both as practical fuel and as decor to impress guests. This achievement was particularly noteworthy in their village, where collecting firewood was considered an important part of a respectable girl's daily duties.

But despite her reputation as a skilled firewood collector, Nyasema longed for something more. Her longing for education was like a seed planted deep within her, and she watered it with her determination to learn. The knowledge that she could be doing more with her life fueled her every day. She desired to attend school. A constant ache in her heart, especially when she saw other children making their way to class. And so, one day, she made a bold decision that would change her life forever.

One day, Nyasema decided to take matters into her own hands, walking to the school and registering herself. On her way back home, she carried firewood with her to disguise her true purpose. Every day, she continued this ruse, pretending to collect firewood in the morning and bringing some back with her when she returned from school in the afternoon. It was a daring and risky game she played, but one that was fueled by her passion and determination to learn.

As the days passed, Nyasema's clandestine academic pursuits remained undetected by her parents. It was only when one of her teachers visited her family to commend her academic achievements that the truth was finally revealed. Her father, initially skeptical of the teacher's claims, was taken aback upon learning that Nyasema was indeed a student and one of the brightest in her class.

Upon being confronted by her father, Nyasema had no choice but to come clean about her secret school attendance. With a sense of unwavering loyalty and determination, she explained to him that she had managed to balance her academic responsibilities with her household duties. Her father, impressed by her courage and dedication, agreed to let her continue attending school, albeit under probationary observation.

Despite the additional responsibilities placed upon her shoulders, Nyasema remained committed to her academic pursuits and her familial duties. She diligently carried out her chores every day, ensuring that the cows were milked and the calves were cared for. Her keen attention to detail and natural ability to care for animals was not lost on her parents, who recognized her gift and praised her for it.

"So, after school and on weekends, I had a list of chores to accomplish. Every evening, I had to milk the cows and take care of the calves, making sure none of the goats or sheep wandered off while grazing. On weekends, I would take them to the verdant meadows in the forest, where they could feast on long grasses. During weekdays, my brother would take care of them."

"In the forest, I would observe the animals and determine which goats were pregnant or about to give birth. More often than not, I was fortunate during my duty and would return home with new calves that I had mid-wifed. It was as if God had blessed my hands since my childhood. My father was always delighted and would tell me that my hands were pure. Even my mother, who was a traditional midwife, was impressed when she learned that I was not afraid to handle such things. She thought I had inherited her gift."

"Ah, those were truly the good old days," my mother fondly remi-nisced. "In the lush forest with the cattle, my friends and I would spend most of our time playing games like *rede* and *mdako*. Despite being the youngest, I was known for my wit and intelligence, but my honesty was often met with disdain by my peers. If we agreed to do something, I would always make sure to tell my parents the truth. I recall a time when some girls convinced me that we should slaughter a lamb, and while I was hesi-tant, I didn't argue against their idea. I was small and not as independent as the other girls, after all."

"We went ahead and slaughtered the lamb in the bush, hoping to keep it a secret from our parents. However, we were left with more sheep meat than we could handle. We roasted most of it over the fire, but still, there was too much left. The bigger girls insisted that we finish it and hide the skin to erase the evidence. I ate and ate, and I thought I was going to be sick. But we had to finish the meat, there was no other way," she chuckled.

"To make matters worse, the lamb we slaughtered belonged to my parents. The girls suggested that we should also slaughter one of our own lambs to cover our tracks, thinking that my father wouldn't notice one missing lamb amidst our sizable herd. I was nervous, but how do you go against your friends?"

"The problem was that the sheep meat is fatty, and it was too much for us to finish. We made a fire and roasted most of it, but still, we couldn't eat all of it. The older girls insisted that we must finish the meat and hide the skin to erase the evidence. We kept eating until we were full and sick. But what could we do? The meat had to be finished," she chuckled.

"There was another problem for me. The lamb we slaughtered belonged to my parents. The girls wanted us to slaughter one of our own lambs so that I wouldn't speak out. Somehow, they thought because we had so many sheep, my father wouldn't notice a missing lamb. I was nervous, but how could I go against my friends?

"I remember returning home with the cattle that evening, trying to appear normal. My father, as usual, quietly went through his flock, registering with his eyes one animal after another. As they say, 'you can lie about anything to a blind man, but not about his walking stick.' My father's flock was like a blind man's walking stick to him. At that time, I had hurriedly walked into my mother's house. Then, I heard my dad calling out, 'Nyasema! Nyasema . . .'

"I came out running, 'Yes, dad!' I knew at that moment that I was done for."

"What happened to the fat lamb?" my father asked, his tone grave.

"Which one?" I pretended not to know, trying to avoid the inevitable conversation.

"The fat lamb, Nyasema," he said, his voice growing sterner.

I considered denying any knowledge of it, but then I realized it was not unusual for a sheep or cow to go missing. "It wasn't me," I said, "They slaughtered it."

"Who are they?" my father demanded, his anger rising.

"The other girls did," I confessed, feeling guilty for going along with their scheme, "They didn't want me to tell you, and they forced me to agree with them."

"To my surprise, my father was not angry after I told him everything. I think he took that as a sign of trust," she said. "Being the youngest among the group of girls and always honest, my father trusted me even more after that incident. From that day on, I was allowed to attend school with no conditions."

"In school, I excelled in my studies. My school days went very well. I could read, write, and do math. Some of the students even asked me to teach them how to read and write. The classes were easy for me, and my teachers were impressed by my achievements. I always scored high grades on all my exams—even when I competed with boys, I defeated them in the final scores. When I came home, I would impress my dad by how I could now count the number of cattle we had and showed him how I could write his name."

"As months and years passed in primary school, my teacher told my father, 'If she continues this way, she will get very far.' It was intended as a compliment, but my father did not take it that way. He saw it as a threat, a warning that I might become too educated to stay with him. He decided that if I passed the final exam and was accepted into middle school, he would not allow me to go, believing it would distance me even further from him."

"Primary school lasted only four years at the time. The morning of the final exam, my father called me into his room and sat me down. He looked me in the eyes and said, 'Look! I understand that your teachers like you. I know there is nothing you cannot do at school. That is how your teacher speak of you. They say you are the best student. But I will not let you go to middle school.'"

"Now listen to me, and listen carefully," her father said sternly, his eyes piercing into mine. "I will not allow my only daughter to be taken away by the missionaries and their schools. You cannot leave me. We are now growing old, and you need to stay here and start your own family. Haven't you learned enough already?" he asked rhetorically, his voice tinged with bitterness.

"This is what I want you to do," my grandfather said to my mother, his words heavy with authority. "When you go to the examination today, I want you to mark 'no' for 'yes,' and 'yes' for 'no.' Don't you dare answer those questions truthfully, and never come back home if you do," he emphasized, his tone leaving no room for negotiation.

"I felt as though a sharp, piercing blade had been plunged into my heart. Those were the most difficult words a traditional young woman like me could hear from her father. I was in a state of perplexity," my mother continued. "I loved and respected my parents, and I would never dare to defy my father," she added. Therefore, not wanting to disappoint her father, Nyasema had realized that her academic efforts had come to an end. She left that morning and approached the examination with a heavy heart. "The questions were incredibly simple. I knew I could have scored 100%," she recounted. "But with every word, I heard my father's voice ringing in my ears: 'if you do, never come back.' I couldn't bring myself to write a single word. I left my exam paper blank and walked home, defeated."

Following the exam, the incredulous teachers were at a loss to comprehend Nyasema's inexplicable failure. "It is simply inconceivable that Nyasema would not pass," they declared. Even Nyasema herself could not fathom obtaining a perfect zero. Despite the failure, the teachers persisted in their belief that Nyasema possessed immense potential and urged her to attend the middle school. In a last-ditch effort, they went to her father's house and implored him to reconsider, regardless of the exam's results. However, her father refused to listen, staunchly standing his ground and turning the teachers away like a lion warding off intruders.

That was it. When the time came, Nyasema was initiated into the mysteries and traditions of womanhood. She delved deeply into the arts, perfecting her singing and refining her dancing abilities. Nyasema's passion for education became overshadowed by the conflict between her loyalty to her cultural traditions and her desire to be a free woman. Unfortunately, those two—loyalty and freedom—are not meant to co-exist.

Time eventually came, and my mother was married to my father. Many years later, the pain of abandoning her education was evident in her unwavering support for her seven children. "I am astounded to witness kids quitting school nowadays!" she often remarked. At times, she would gaze at the world around her with a longing expression and say, "I wish I had been born in this age, an age where women have the freedom to choose." Then she would turn bitter, muttering, "But girls these days are worthless! They have all the liberty they desire and yet they squander it foolishly." In our days, girls were born to become responsible women," a statement that I struggled to comprehend.

XII

-

A Bird with no Wings

—

Nʏᴀsᴇᴍᴀ's ᴇxᴘᴇʀɪᴇɴᴄᴇ ʜɪɢʜʟɪɢʜᴛ ᴛʜᴏsᴇ of many. However, her profession came with another profession. That was besides being a midwife. To understand it, I must first bring up Sophia's tale. In Arimi proverbs, Sophia would be referred as "has skipped over the pee to land on the poop!" My mother would say, "*amejitaakiaa mwenyewe*—she has coveted herself."

Sophia is my cousin's wife. She and I shared a little secret. I officially met her when she was dating my cousin. I was probably less than ten at the time and, I am not certain I had enough knowledge of what "dating" entailed. Somehow, Sophia was the one who introduced me to their relationship.

I was on my way to buy kerosene. The kiosk was about two or three miles from our home. To beat the sunset, I had decided to take a short cut—the road that went across a ditch before connecting with *ifanda ra manyunchwe*. In the shrubs, the day light has already dimmed and darkness fast approached. Yet my mother had insisted "come back before the sunset!" Somewhat parents never realized what they needed in the kitchen until it was late.

With my bare feet, I hurriedly ran in a jogging pace in unpaved cow path. I passed by the *mpimbi* rocks where kids used to spend their afternoon to chase lizards while grassing cows. Behind rocks was a shallow *mukatokato* well that was the main source of a drinking water. But the well depended on the rain, so in the summer, it was mostly dry. The well was seated by a high rock where in the afternoon, we played a sledding game that often tore our pants, in front of which was a *mukatokato* tree that offered some shade for water fetchers.

Sophia, who I believe was in her peak of puberty, was hiding under some shrubs between the sledding rock and *Muhuve* tree. I did not see her at first and when I did, I could not help but to notice her "hunt" mode. I walked pass her with no intent to know why she was out there by herself in that place and that time of the day. But I think, she saw me first as she had prepared such a seductive smile. And as I walked passed her, she called; "Hey you!" in a whispering voice. "Come!" she gestured in unavoidable tenderness. Somehow the way she called, told me, even in that youngish age, that she was expecting someone.

"Where are you going?" she asked, as if to hide her amorous expression.

"I am going to buy kerosene"

"Kerosene! Who did you see on your way here? Have you seen Rama—Rama your cousin? Was he home?" she asked.

"Rama?" I repeated.

"Yes."

"Yes, he is home, why?" I asked. "I saw him at *Ihanja* with other boys" I added without waiting for her response.

My aunt's house was next to my parents' house. When I left, Rama, his brother, and other young men were outside roasting popcorns at *Ihanja* (by a cows' fence).

"Good! Let's make a deal," Sophia cunningly whispered.

"What deal?" I asked curiously.

"When you return home, can you go to Rama and let him know that I am waiting here? I will give you something—something really good," she insisted while trying to robe my childish trust. I did not know exactly what was happening between them, but even as a teen I noticed there was something fishy going on. But kids being kids, I agreed and almost forgot about it.

I went on to buying kerosine and on my way back I did not come the same way so I was not sure Sophia was still waiting. It was after I walked by my aunt's house when I remembered about her. I got home, presented the kerosene to my mom and ran out to check if Rama and his friends were still there. They had gone inside. When I got in, I went straight to where Rama was seated. Somehow, when he saw me, he became suspicious about what message I was carrying. To this day, I still cannot tell how he sensed it, because the way he looked at me was as if he had smelled of something confidential coming.

I lowered myself to whisper to his ear. And casually told him, "Sophia is waiting." But as a kid, I think my voice trailed off. He cautiously pinched my hand to shush me and pulled me away from the group of seniors. I guess I was not far from spilling the beans. "You are stupid! What are you doing?" he told me outside. He looked a bit terrified in his voice but kept a brave smile. "I wanted to let you know she is out there waiting! Who is she to you anyway?" I asked him in a charming voice. "But you don't want everyone to know . . . do you? You must keep this between us, don't tell anybody— okay?" he warned me in a friendly manner. "Okay!" I replied while smiling.

That was the beginning of my knowing that Rama and Sophia were dating. As a teenager, after that incident, I forgot all about it. To this day, my cousin and I have never revisited this story.

Some days had passed, and I forgot all about it again. One morning, when I was still in bed in a shared room with my dad, my aunt (Rama's mom) knocked at the door. It was still early, about 6:00 a.m., I think. She wanted to talk to my father. I pretended to be asleep at the time to give myself an opportunity to absorb the grown-ups' talk. After *sayu*—a lengthy traditional greeting, my aunt told my dad that there was a problem. To my aunt, dad was her immediate older brother. Uncle Muna was technically the oldest but he lived in a far village to be reached. That left dad to solve all issues pertaining his siblings in the village.

"What is it?" my dad asked my aunt.

"The youngsters got themselves into some troubles," she said in plural form. Parents in my culture often use a plural form even when referring to one individual. Somehow this attests to the fact that the problem of one child is the problem for all. In this case, her inclusive language did not help me at all, on whether the one in trouble was Rama, his brother, or both. My dad paid more attention: "what happened?" As if he knew exactly who was the person of interest.

It turned out that that kerosene night, Rama had sneaked Sophia into the house. By the house, I mean *idemu*—the boys' house. She had been in *idemu* for almost a month, and nobody except Rama, his brother, and their friends knew about it. And the worst thing was Sophia was currently pregnant.

Among Arimi, as boys mature, they cease to share the house with their mothers. They get their *idemu*—the boys' hut. These boys' huts are only for men. Rarely would women or parents try to enter the *idemu* without a good reason. Thus, what happens in *idemu* remains between men. For my aunt, she was a single mother. She had lost her husband a long time ago, and thus she would never have known what went on in the boys' ghetto.

Rama, who had finished primary school, was probably on his seventeenth or eighteenth years. So technically he was mature but not enough to get married. He was in that age of knowing—or rather exploring what girls tasted like. One of those girls happened to be Sophia.

As we know in these stories, their intimacy grew deeper between the two, and instead of meeting behind rocks, they decided to move in the house. Then, Rama decided to bring Sophia home secretively. After he brought her in, the question remained how to take care of her without his mother knowing. Boys never came short of plans. Rama pretended that he was sick—or at least not feeling well. That way, he would not join with the family for meals at their mother's living room. His food would be sent to his bedroom instead.

His younger sibling was part of this scheme—he brought him food. But that food was meant to feed Rama and Sophia. Of course they changed the tricks and came out, but then they would sneak in the leftovers to Sophia when their mother was away. That was how they stayed alive in there for such a long time. But as they say, "A honey taster never tasted once." Rama was snared by a young girl to easily to let her go. When they were found out, Sophia and Rama had already screwed up.

Sophia was kind of a runaway girl. At a time her parents had lost track of her. They didn't know where she was. She had dropped out of primary school early on and since then her life had been between Mtinko and cities. She would take the bus some days and disappear for several days or months. Then she would appear to one of her sisters in the city. Some days parents assumed she had gone to visit her uncles who lived in different places. If it was then as it is now, mobile phones would have helped, but back then there was no way to check where she was. After all, her parents were careless, as people would say. As long as there was no police report that a girl was found dead, I guess they didn't care about her whereabouts.

The problem emerged when Sophia wanted to come out from the boys' hut. Some weeks had passed. When Rama had got enough of her and wanted to release her, she probably, knowing that she had missed her period, refused to leave. She found out that she was pregnant. According to my aunt, as she told my dad, Sophia threatened Rama that if she was forced out, she would commit suicide.

It is a shame among Arimi, as it is among other African cultures, for a girl to get pregnant before marriage. "I will not be able to show myself to my parents this way," Sophia was reported saying. "I better die," my cousin explained later. Although I sometimes think that she played that card to win Rama for a husband. Anyhow! Rama and his younger brother had to choose between forcing her out or to come clean. When they decided that they could not get her out forcibly, they then had to explain this shit to their mother.

"*Wazazi ni jalala*"—parents are like a trash can, my aunt said to my dad. "We are forced to take all the trash!" she added angrily. Although I was pretending to be asleep, I was fully awake, absorbing everything my aunt told Dad. As she spoke, everything came to a circle from the day I met Sophia. "I had played a part in this mess," I told myself. I lazily rolled on the bed as if to announce that I was waking up. "What can be done now?" my aunt asked my dad without caring that I was awake. This question was more about traditional measures around Sophia's pregnancy. Aunt wanted dad to advise on what customs must be observed to neutralize the situation.

"Well! I think there is nothing to worry about," dad began in a very calm voice. "First, as for the girl—there is no need to keep her inside," meaning in *idemu*—the boys' hut. While my aunt sounded so terrified and angry, my dad was so calm and relaxed. He proceeded, "both of them are grown-up enough, I think they have—I think they chose to start a family. They should be able to start their home—we will let them get married," dad concluded.

"But what about the girl's parents? Are we not related?" my aunt asked. "We are . . . but they have already broken that barrier. Let me see, our clan's connection is through her dad who is the son of *Ntue*, *Ntue* is the son of *Malwe* of . . . the connection is very distant—and Rama would be considered as Sophia's distant brother—but since they have wrecked it, let's see." Dad went on and on as if doing some math problems on how and what cultural norms' and traditions' tension must be solved. He continued; "normally in this circumstance, her parents would ask us to pay a *njughuda*—penalty. And that should be a goat or two. So that is what we should plan for. That should resolve the *ndughu*—relation crisis. Then, we pay for dowry. And she is a cheap girl—we would refuse to give them more than three cows, one of which can be paid now, and we will tell them that the second and third will be paid later. That will allow them to get married, and after they are married, it doesn't matter whether we choose to pay the remaining dowry or not. That should be it." To my ears, my dad's approach on this case was beyond impressive.

Going to my aunt's house was my first thing after I woke up that morning. As I approached the house, Sophia was shyly sitting in the living room of the main house, already helping my aunt to prepare some breakfast. She was no longer in the hiding. As she saw me, she gave me such a sideway quick gaze as if to say 'you knew all about this.' But she pretended to ignore me and continued with her chore. I almost busted in laughter, reading her mind. Seeing how she pretended to not know me was funny. But I held back my boyish giggling and backed up to leave the house.

I went to Rama instead. He was in *idemu*. This time he acted like a real man—a man with a wife, although I cannot say he was confident of this new role. As I walked the door, I jocularly whispered to his ear, "Why didn't you tell me?" "About what?" he whispered back, although his familiar smile indicated that he knew what I was referring to. "Don't you guys know that I was the one who connected you?" I asked jocularly again. Rama chuckled and kicked me on my butt childishly. So that was how Sophia became *muramu ane*—my sister in-law and how they got married. There was no proper wedding.

As previously mentioned, families like Sophia's are unfortunately viewed with disdain, particularly among the Arimi. Their girls are regarded as undisciplined for being allowed to wander freely, leading to criticisms such as "*wanaruka ruka*" (jumping around). Therefore, what had befallen Sophia not only brought shame upon herself but also reflected poorly on her family. As the saying goes, "when a mad woman walks naked, it is her family that should feel shame."

The scandal quickly spread throughout the village, and in such situations, it is often the girl and her mother who bear the brunt of the blame. Several months later, there were murmurs among the women that Sophia had not undergone initiation, leading to rumors that she was not circumcised. The belief was that her behavior was a result of her lack of adherence to traditional moral standards. Her conduct, such as showing up unannounced at a man's house, was deemed unacceptable. Therefore, she would need to be tamed to fit into the clan's expectations, or she would need to become a wife.

The form of female circumcision practiced by the Arimi involves the removal of a girl's clitoris and part of her labia minora. This ritual was originally conducted as part of a woman's preparation for marriage, among other things, as part of her initiation rite of passage after puberty. However, female circumcision is currently banned in Tanzania. Despite this, the Arimi and many other cultures in Tanzania continue to practice it secretly by performing genital cutting, often avoiding the initiation ceremony altogether. To avoid detection by government officials, the practice is sometimes conducted as early as birth, leaving many girls unaware of what has been done to them.

It is a widely held belief within the Arimi community, and many other cultures in Tanzania, that an uncircumcised woman, regardless of her age, is considered immature. She is viewed as a child who is unable to fit into the world of cultural women and is deemed unclean. This is because the traditional education that cultural women undergo is rigorous, and circumcision is considered a crucial symbol of their maturity and readiness for marriage, among other things. Therefore, the absence of circumcision signifies a lack of adherence to the traditional moral standards that cultural women are expected to uphold. This belief is deeply ingrained in these cultures, and it continues to be upheld to this day.

Sophia, however, serves as an exemplification of the Swahili proverb, "*Mshika mbili zote humponyoka*"—a two-sided grabber loses all. This, I must assert, is a post-colonial phenomenon prevalent among African cultures. It is a struggle between African and Western worldviews and has been documented by many scholars. Ngugi wa Thiong'o's *The River Between* serves as a perfect example of this phenomenon, although in reversed roles. In the novel, Chege urges his son Waiyaki to attend the mission school, learn the wisdom and secrets of the white man, but not adopt his vices. Waiyaki is expected to explore this foreign worldview while remaining true to his people and ancient customs.

Unfortunately, Waiyaki falls in love with an uncircumcised daughter of a Christian preacher—Nyambura. They find themselves caught between two worlds—on one hand, Waiyaki cannot marry the uninitiated woman, while on the other hand, he cannot fully be embraced in the missionary family as he himself is "unclean" (not baptized). Waiyaki's people consider this a betrayal, and he ultimately meets the same fate as traditionalist leaders and antagonistic forces on his conflicted "old-new" ways of navigation.

He fails to preserve his tradition while also being unable to fully acquire the modern way of life. The opposite can also be true for Nyambura.

Although Waiyaki and Nyambura symbolize a reconciliation model, Ngugi wa Thiong'o in his book wanted to challenge and manifest the tension between the two coexisting traditions in African cultures. From the very title, *The River Between*, Ngugi poses a critique of this phenomenon that amounts to metaphorically sitting between the river that separates two ridges in conflict—indigenous culture and European culture. Since the latter tradition aimed to erase the former, Ngugi uses Waiyaki as a symbol of indecision, suggesting that post-colonial Africa by being unable to reconcile two ridges is mounting to "drowning."

The phenomenon of uprootedness in Africa is a complex issue, often tied to the influence of Westernization. In Africa, many individuals who have been exposed to Westernization are presented with a choice: to abandon their African roots and embrace Christian values or the modern education system. This shift in identity is often rooted in a view that considers African systems to be outdated and inferior to Western ones. As a result, there is a disconnection between the traditional African identity and the Western-influenced identity, causing a sense of cultural dissonance because an attempt to detach was embedded within a colonial imagination that suggested that one cannot remain true to both "African" and "Christian" or "educated" identities simultaneously. It also implied that African values are always outdated and barbaric, requiring replacement with so-called "civilized" Western values.

I must therefore be careful on how I present these stories. It is important to recognize that African cultures , like any culture, are not static but rather dynamic and evolving. They have adapted and changed over time, and can continue to do so while still retaining their essence and core values. The coexistence of African and Western values is possible, and can lead to a stronger and more vibrant cultural identity. Rather than rejecting or denying the African heritage, I still believe that we Africans can still embrace it while struggling to build a better and just society.

Each approach we take must foster a sense of pride in one's cultural identity and create a more inclusive and diverse society. It is crucial to recognize and celebrate the values of our traditions and perspectives, and to reject the notion that injustices presented in this book represent the inherently inferiority of African cultures to Western values or how African have always treated their women.

The "duality" nature presented in Sophia's account, creates what others have called a "cultural dissonance." Some have associated this dissonance with the dilemma between (re)defining the "distinctive African personality" and modifying the colonial legacy. In my reading and observing of these tensions, I see the ambition to build a programmatic society that is contextual, thus bringing the relevant aspects of modern life in, where cultural values are revisited but not negated.

I couldn't help but wonder what would happen now that Sophia was married but still not circumcised. Would women still forcibly grab her between the thighs, as is traditionally done? I wasn't entirely certain, but I had my doubts. Perhaps Sophia, with her sense of modernity, had escaped this tradition for good, or maybe she had only delayed the inevitable. After all, she was now married and soon to have a baby. Despite my hopeful thoughts, I understood that tradition held great power, and most women in our culture would go to great lengths to uphold it. It remained to be seen what Sophia's future held in this regard.

****

The prayer of betrothal recited by *munyoronga matya* epitomizes the unyielding devotion of Arimi people to their deities. They devoutly direct their supplications towards the sumptuous moon and implore the creator, *Matunda*, to bring forth all things in twos—male and female babies who will mature, wed, and nurture one another, like a herdsman tending to his flock. "Let there be a bull and a heifer, a ram and a ewe, a billy goat and a nanny goat, a jack and a jenny, a hen and a rooster, a female pup and a kitten. And let the forest swarm with an abundance of wild animals, each male and female. It is fitting and proper for all creatures to prosper and propagate," the recitation goes.

This recitation exude an aura of power that permeated all of creation. As the children woke, stretching their backs to the sound of the pillars of the kraal, some rubbing their bleary eyes, still shaken by remnants of a nightmare, fathers arose with the expectation that their sons would soon become men, while mothers perched on their *mwango*, praying for their daughters to flourish into womanhood.

Meanwhile, in the seemingly mundane village of Mtinko, the moon had receded and the sun beamed down, promising a splendid day. The women scurried off to collect water as per their usual routine, while the men huddled around the *ihanja* fire, anticipating the call for *ikoko*, their morning meal, before embarking on the day's cattle grazing. Snotty-nosed children, their bellies empty and their voices hoarse from their morning cries, trailed their way to their grandparents' *makita*, eager for fresh milk. Although Nyasema's home bustled with activity, she was nowhere to be found.

Amidst the thrum of daily life, a group of skilled women had congregated around a small wooden bed, covered in a cowhide, situated within a hut. They had spent the night here, for Sophia was giving birth. This was my aunt's dwelling. They had gathered to lend their assistance.

I only learned of this after I returned home that afternoon, having been playing outside with other boys. Hungry, I arrived at our house, only to have my mother greet me and inquire, "Have you seen the baby?" My excitement was palpable as I responded, "A baby! Whose baby?" "Sophia's. She has a newborn," my mother replied. "Incredible!" I exclaimed, racing off to my aunt's home, completely forgetting about my hunger. My mother had sent me away to keep me occupied while she prepared lunch.

I was determined to see the baby before lunch. As a child, I adored holding newborns, and my mother knew of my fondness for them. At one point, I had even aspired to become a midwife like her, though that dream never materialized. As I arrived at my aunt's house, my cousin Rama sat outside against the wall, grinning from ear to ear. He was now a father—to a baby girl!

I paid him no attention and walked straight into the house. Inside, the women were merrily chattering away in the dimly lit room. Some sang, some yodeled, and some danced—everyone was in a celebratory mood, except for Sophia. Nonetheless, it was a good day.

I noticed Sophia lying on the side of the bed, trying to look strong despite her lack of genuine joy. The pangs of childbirth were still evident on her youthful face. Becoming a woman was said to come with enduring pain. Even when in agony, Sophia could only whimper quietly. She lay stretched out, as if to deceive herself that she was an adult, but in truth, she was still a young girl. Her mother-in-law (my aunt) bellowed at her, "Don't be foolish! Sing softly!" Crying from the pain of childbirth was a source of shame for women. Enduring pain was what initiation had prepared women for, and the initiated woman was supposed to be stronger. But Sophia had not yet been initiated, and so she could only grit her teeth in agony. She tried to join the women in song, perhaps to ease her pain with the distraction, but to no avail.

As I settled onto the three-legged stool, my aunt gently placed the baby into my waiting hands. "Your grandmother," she pointed out, adjusting the cloth that covered the infant. Isia, as she was named, after our grandmother. As the saying goes, "*Kitanda hakizai haramu*"—the bed does not give birth to unclean. The pure thing was in my hands, innocent of how she entered this world. Isia was a darling little thing, with chubby cheeks like her mother, destined to grow into a woman like everyone else. Later, as I emerged from the room, I announced to the other boys outside, "We have a new baby in the neighborhood! Our grandmother is born!"

Later that evening, my mother divulged something strange to my father. In my young mind, I couldn't say I had seen this one coming. Whenever my mother acted as a midwife for a woman, she would always update my dad on how the process went. I enjoyed listening in on these briefings, and over time, I had developed a desire to become a midwife or doctor, just like her. But this time, there was something more to their conversation. "They took it away," my mother started, as if in the midst of a familiar dialogue. "They did! How?" my dad asked. The entire exchange sounded like a code to me, and I couldn't understand what my mom was referring to, although I suspected it had something to do with Sophia. As usual, I pretended to be asleep, hoping to hear more of their conversation.

"Yes, they did," my mother insisted, using the plural tense once again. I still couldn't comprehend who "they" were or what "they" had done to someone. "They had to do it during her labor pains. Did you think they would let her keep it?" my mother added, as if distancing herself from whatever had happened. "I see!" my dad replied, followed by a long pause. The conversation left me feeling left out, but at least I knew whatever had occurred had happened to Sophia. But who were these "they," and what had they taken? I wondered. As my parents continued to converse, I learned that the "thing" had meant something to Sophia. Eventually, I understood that my mom was referring to Sophia's clitoris. Mom added, "She will settle down now," implying that Sophia would no longer exchange men like she used to since her clitoris had been removed.

I was astounded by this revelation. Sophia had been genitally mutilated during childbirth. She had escaped the tradition by embracing modern ways of life, but unfortunately, her restlessness had brought her back to the same tradition she had despised. In Arimi culture, they say, "*Igutrambaa guinto igusuka*," which means, "regardless of how high a bird might attempt to fly, it will eventually return to the ground, and its feathers will be harvested for arrows." That was what my mom referred to as *"amejitakia mwenyewe"*—she sought this for herself."

It seemed that Sophia couldn't fully embrace either modern or cultural ways of life. If she had chosen education, and not to have engaged with man in such age, she would probably have escaped these atrocities. But she dropped out of school and married unplanned. She had "jumped over the pee to land on the poo."

****

Did I not assert that womanhood is a product of nurture, not nature? It cannot be reduced to biology alone, nor can it be attributed solely to natural factors. It is "nature via nurture," as one author once wrote. Even in the early days of human society, we had already departed from a purely natural existence, and today we are shaped by the cultural environments in which we live. Our identity as men and women is a complex interplay of nature and nurture, but culture plays an increasingly significant role in shaping who we are. While early humans may have created culture, it now creates us in profound ways.

Female genital mutilation (FGM) is one of several rites of passage that women in some Tanzanian cultures, including the Arimi people, undergo on their journey to womanhood. While FGM is a particularly egregious example of gender-based injustices, it is by no means the only one. It is important to note that not all cultures in Tanzania practice FGM, and this book is not exclusively focused on this issue. Each culture has its unique customs for shaping the identities of men and women. However, for those cultures that do practice FGM, it is just one component of a broader set of rituals. To fully understand the extent of this practice, I must recount a specific encounter I had.

A few weeks after my ordination, just prior to departing for Igengu, I paid Malewo a visit during his final month of internship. To reach his abode, I boarded a public bus from Singida to Ikungi area. By the time I arrived, it was already late and Malewo was taken aback by my unexpected visit. I appeared fatigued, having traveled for hundreds of miles on a dusty road, crammed in the bus among fellow passengers. But more notably, I was profoundly vexed, and this was clearly evident from my countenance. "What's the matter?" Malewo inquired. "The ridiculous bus conductor," I fumed. "What did he do?" he probed.

As it happened, I had purchased a bus ticket and paid for a full-price seat, only to discover later that it had been sold to another passenger. This was a common occurrence. Bus conductors often entice people to pay for a "VIP seat" only to later find out that it has been sold to multiple people. Consequently, on that day, I was forced to stand in the cramped aisle of a minibus for over two hours, holding on to the pipe to Makiungu. I was smacking my lips furiously. "If I weren't a pastor, I'd have killed that guy," I lamented to Malewo. "How can they make me stand throughout the entire journey? I have the ticket—it's mine!" I ranted, as though Malewo were somehow involved in the deception. Rather than commiserate with me, Malewo simply chuckled in his usual "don't take life too seriously" manner. "Come here," he beckoned, giving me a hug. "We've got better things to do," he added, taking my backpack from my shoulder.

I assumed I was going to rest, but Malewo had other plans. "We're not staying," he declared. "Not staying?" I exclaimed. "Nope! You caught me on my way out to visit Mwangi, so you must come along," Malewo replied nonchalantly, slipping his shoes back on. "Who's Mwangi?" I inquired. "Just come with me," he retorted breezily, heading for the door. "But bro . . ." I began to protest. "I know you're tired, but this visit is of utmost importance," Malewo stated firmly, brandishing a key in his hand. Before I could argue, Malewo and I were already en route to Mwangi's abode.

I had never met Mwangi before, but Malewo briefed me on him on the way. As it turned out, Mwangi had summoned Malewo to discuss his daughter Joyce, who had returned home from her husband. Even though Malewo was just an intern pastor, Mwangi regarded him as a full pastor, or even his son from afar. Upon our arrival, Joyce, whom I had also never met, greeted us with *magahi*, a customary drink that every guest must be offered. As we took our first sips, I overheard Mwangi whisper to Malewo, "That's your sister, for whom I requested your presence. She's back from her husband's place." Mwangi then excused himself to give us some privacy in the living room.

Before delving deeper into the story, I must mention that blending in with the people of Tanzania is not a difficult feat. For the Arimi tribe, all it takes is to know the customary greeting "sayu" to become acclimated. This unique salutation served as a bridge between strangers, instantly bringing them together as if they were longtime acquaintances. "Sayu" involved exchanging details about one's background, such as information on parents, siblings, clan, and connections with the person you're conversing with. This ritual took place when Malewo and I sat down at Mwangi's house, allowing Joyce and her father to know exactly who I was and how we were distantly related.

Following "Sayu," Malewo, Joyce, and I transitioned from being pastors to friends, and from strangers to relatives. However, during our conversation, I sensed that something was amiss. Joyce seemed uncomfortable speaking freely, and Malewo was struggling to get her to open up. Realizing this, I suggested to Malewo that we move the conversation to his office, and he agreed.

The following day, Joyce arrived at Malewo's living room office, and although she was initially reserved, she gradually began to open up. Later, she confided in me that she had been hesitant to speak during our initial encounter because her younger brother was taking a nap, and she was worried he might overhear our conversation. Given the sensitivity of the matter, her concerns were understandable.

When we met Joyce, she had been married for three years and was the mother of a two-year-old. From an outsider's perspective, it was difficult to gauge what she was going through. Her father had informed Malewo that her marriage was on the rocks, but we needed to hear it from Joyce herself.

Malewo, whom I had known since his adolescence, possessed an innate talent for utilizing humor to alleviate the tension in serious discussions. He was the kind of individual who could temporarily dispel anyone's problems with his charismatic anecdotes and witty remarks. Regardless of the nature of the conversation, Malewo possessed a unique ability to make people feel ill at ease initially, before they eventually warmed up to his charismatic personality. I found that his approach was unconventional, but highly effective. I was pleased to discover that he hadn't lost his sense of humor even after he had become a pastor.

As Joyce approached Malewo's office chair, the first question he posed to her was shockingly personal: "Okay Joyce! Tell us about your sexual life with your husband?" I couldn't help but feel that the query was highly inappropriate. "Where did this question come from?" Joyce mumbled. Malewo continued, "I know you have a daughter, but how much sex do you have with your husband?" He thrust these enormous and intrusive questions upon a woman who hadn't even acclimatized to discussing her marriage.

"What do you mean, pastor?" Joyce stammered.

"I want to know about your sexual life. You don't make love with your husband, do you?" Malewo pressed.

"Who told you . . . my hus . . ." Joyce struggled to find words, but Malewo cut in, bursting into tears of laughter.

"Sit down, Joyce. Don't take your pastor seriously," I intervened. Joyce managed a forced smile and found comfort in settling into her chair.

She let out a deep exhale as she shifted her chair to the side. "To me, you are our younger sister. I hope you wouldn't mind talking to us," I offered.

"No problem, I know," she replied with a smile. "Tell us what's going on," I urged her.

"My husband doesn't love me. He drinks too much these days, more than before. I think he has another woman," Joyce confessed, becoming emotional as she spoke.

She went on to discuss several issues, including her husband coming home late, spending money on drinking, and harassing her, among other things. However, she didn't mention anything about her sex life, as Malewo had asked.

After she finished sharing her version of events, Malewo returned to his earlier question: "You didn't tell us anything about your sexual life."

I understand that for some, these questions might seem offensive or intrusive, and I would agree that they are highly personal. However, after becoming accustomed to discussing these issues, and with the knowledge of the culture, one can come to appreciate that Malewo had a valid reason for asking these questions. While Malewo's approach was quite direct, his questions were pertinent to the circumstances.

Joyce showed some hesitancy at first, but eventually found the courage to speak her mind. "When I was getting married, I thought sex was going to be wonderful. People and books always talked about sex as if it was magical, pleasurable, and so on," she began. "But . . ."

"But it wasn't like that when you got married," Malewo interjected.

"No, it wasn't like that," Joyce agreed. "These days, I just wish I could be left alone. I think I am more comfortable with my daughter's company than seeing my husband in bed every night. If I am not getting anything out of it, what's the point? Maybe if I want another baby."

Joyce revealed her feelings about sex, which were clearly negative. At one point, she even stated, "Now I'm thinking, 'What a foolish woman to initiate sex!'" in response to Malewo's question about whether she knew anything about orgasms or would initiate sex.

"Let's address that first," I suggested to her. From there, Malewo and I began a "sex" class.

Women like Joyce are the quintessential embodiments of their culture, shaped by tradition and steeped in its customs. As my mother used to say, "she was a woman." For people of her upbringing, sex was a taboo topic, shrouded in shame and secrecy. It was a duty to be performed in a dimly lit room, eyes shut tight, solely for the pleasure of one's husband. Girls who indulged in premarital sex were viewed with disdain, likened to a young chameleon treading on thorns. If not cursed, they had to endure public shame to appease society's morals. Girls who underwent female genital mutilation, on the other hand, were deemed fit to become wives; they could not be restless.

Scholars have delved into the meaning of circumcision in African cosmology. The practice aimed to "remove something female from the male and something male from the female."[1] Before undergoing the rite, the female's manliness was said to be expressed through her clitoris, while the male's femaleness was embodied in his foreskin. Among the Arimi, the clitoris is referred to as "*mwambolo*," meaning "a small penis."[2] Thus, before circumcision, both genders are considered equally masculine and feminine. These contradictions had to be reconciled. And circumcision would balance the masculinity and femininity within both sexes. For a woman, circumcision involved the removal of her male aspect (the small penis), strengthening her femininity, while for men, it entailed the removal of their femaleness, strengthening their masculinity. For women, however, obedience and sexual desire were not meant to coexist.

Malewo and I were aware of what Joyce lacked. Though initiation into adulthood exposed youths to adulthood, it was intended to neutralize their sexual desires. For women like Joyce, sex was viewed as a taboo subject, and they would say, "I don't think it is something I should ask from a man; I would rather be left alone." In traditional marriages, procreation was the primary goal.

However, Joyce no longer lived in a strictly traditional world. She straddled two worlds—traditional and modern. She had heard and read about sexual pleasure but had never experienced it. As a result, the act lacked any appeal, leading her to push her husband away. She preferred to be left alone. It took a deliberate conversation for Joyce to realize that her

1. Diop, *African Origin of Civilization*, 136.

2. Hilinti, *Gendering Divinities*, 112.

attitudes toward sex were not her fault. Her mother and father had never discussed such matters with her, and she had been left to navigate her own reality as a married woman. In her mind, marriage was a puzzle piece that every woman had to live with; her fate was sealed. A married woman was seen as good as forgotten, especially when it came to issues of intimacy. She only belonged to her marriage; that was her home.

Joyce would not share with her parents what she was lacking in marriage. But no woman would ever dare to complain about not being satisfied in bed let alone to her parents. That fate comes with enduring pains during the act. The practice of genital mutilation, which is meant to distance women from enjoying sex, had unfortunately made them slaves to their own pleasure. Joyce was therefore raised to be the expert of her tradition but unfortunately a foreigner within herself. Her struggle goes deep to a whole misconception that came with being a woman in the marriage. Malewo and I had to undo these taboos.

How would one help a victim of clitoridectomy? After our long conversation, finally, Joyce stood up in our midst and said, "now I understand; my husband might not be that bad. I think I've contributed to the whole thing. Let me go back to my home tomorrow. I think I was ignorant of myself. I want to see if I can work this advice."

I should say that Malewo and I talked with Joyce more as clan's men than as her pastors. The good thing was that both of us shared the same cultural background, the only difference was that Malewo and I were men and Joyce was a woman. Both of us came from the ethnic group that performed female circumcision among other things. Although we didn't ask her, we understood that women like Joyce are genitally mutilated so they see no value in sex. But that was not the end of life; still something else could be done. After that conversation, Joyce left the following morning, and she is still married. Assumably, everything was working in the right direction.

XIII

-

(Un)celebrating Memory

—

TRADITIONS AND CUSTOMS ARE like a fortress, impenetrable from the outside but accessible from within its foundations. This was the driving force behind Deborah's proposition to enlist my mother's expertise in her endeavors. As a staunch traditionalist, my mother and other of her expertise, possessed the code to the cultural secrets that Deborah sought. After Nyasema agreed with some hesitation, Deborah arranged for her and other women to attend a week-long women's empowerment seminar that was held by the ELCT churchwide. When Mama returned, an activist was born from a traditionalist.

That same year, my wife's campaign against female genital mutilation and her fight for women's empowerment garnered widespread attention from the media. Newspaper headlines featured her progress, and her phone was bombarded with calls from different parts of the country, congratulating her and supporting her work. The most memorable call came from the vice chancellor of a university, which later granted her a scholarship for further studies.

Initially, I assisted my wife as her unwilling secretary, organizing logistics for the seminars and preparing educational materials. However, as I transcribed her reports, I became her student. Her accounts were harrowing, describing the trauma women had endured and their feelings towards themselves, their marriages, and their cultures. During one seminar, a woman recounted how her grandmother had mutilated her genital parts when she was a child. Another woman shared how she was circumcised after getting married, causing her to experience pain during sex.

Esther, who was circumcised at the age of twelve, revealed that her clitoris had emerged again. When she was pregnant with her first child, her parents and other women wanted to cut it off, but she was able to protect herself from further mutilation. She had heard about sexual gratification but had never known that was possible.

Another young woman shared her painful experiences with Deborah. She had been married to a man from a region where female genital mutilation was not common, but every time she went to the hospital for delivery, doctors and nurses would ask about her tribe, as they could see that her private parts had been cut. "I feel so embarrassed," she said. "Every time I get pregnant, I have to relive these humiliations. I have even reached a point where I don't want to have children anymore."

Mwajuma also had a tragic experience. After being circumcised, she did not realize that her vagina opening was completely closed during the healing process. She only discovered this after getting married when her husband was unable to penetrate her. She had to be sent back home for a local opening surgery. "I cannot even begin to explain the pain," she said as she teared up.

Yet another young woman spoke of her deep sense of loss and sadness. "I hate everything about myself," she said. Her clitoris and labia minora had been completely removed, leaving her with a "open hole" as she described it. "Anything can get in there," she said. "One day, while working on a farm, a piece of millet got inside me, and I couldn't pull it out. Men and women gathered around me, trying to extract it. They treated me like a piece of meat, digging their fingers into my vagina. I bled profusely, and my private parts swelled up and started to smell. Nobody cared enough to take me to a hospital. It took a month for the millet to come out on its own, and by then, I was badly injured and traumatized."

As the seminars progressed, Deborah observed a shift in the women's attitudes. They became more assertive and aware of their rights, motivated by their own experiences as victims of these injustices. However, there were still obstacles to overcome, as my wife noted. "The key groups we need to engage are local surgeons and men," she explained. Surgeons, some of who were midwives like my mother, were often reluctant to acknowledge their practices. Even in meetings with Deborah, they denied any involvement in the practice, until one finally confessed to almost causing a disability in a young girl. However, due to confidentiality and possible litigation, their identities must remain undisclosed.

Nowadays, Deborah found, the rituals are conducted secretly, either soon after birth or during a woman's labor pains, which is a sad reality, as my wife lamented with a long and tired sigh.

Undeterred, Deborah continued to broaden her outreach efforts, engaging with various groups such as the elderly, youth, and children, separately. She even visited different churches to meet with their administration and organized seminars around church groups. She reached out to all religious groups, not just Christians, to spread the message. Additionally, she began organizing village youth festivals, where youngsters from different places could express themselves through song, poetry, and art, all aimed at raising awareness about the issue. This campaign proved to be highly successful.

Her work was of paramount importance. As for me, I was not beyond her apprentice, learning about the secrets of women in our cultures that I, as a man, would never have known or thought about. What man could ever understand the lived experiences of women? How could I decipher the meaning of *imaa* or *ifaha* rituals? How could I interpret the lyrics and melodies of the moaning songs or understand the movements illustrated in their dances? These were all words and unspoken words that carried with them the weight of a woman's shadow.

In a dreamlike state, I began to discern this shadow that moved with great swiftness. It moved with dynamism, suspense, and uncertainty, and my curiosity and acuity were piqued by its foreshadowing. "What lies behind it?" I asked myself as I gazed upon my wife, mother, sisters, and all the women I encountered.

However, the shadow never halted, always moving, and I endeavored to look through it but was unsuccessful. I was a man in a woman's world, and whatever I saw was only brief glimpses of my masculine ignorance. The invisible was what I could discern. This became the "reality" of their experience within me; the reality that never took a singular form. Just like shadows, realities are never rigid, and they can take on various shapes and meanings as they move towards the unknown.

****

Bibliography

Diop, Cheikh Anta. *The African Origin of Civilization: Myth or Reality*. Translated by Mercer Cook. Chicago: Lawrence Hill Books, 1974.

Hilinti, Syprian. *Gendering Divinities, Endangering Humans? Theological and Anthropological Constructions of Gender, Equality and Ambiguity among Wanyaturu-Iraqw of Tanzania*. Oslo: University of Oslo Press, 2013.

Hughes, Langston. "Harlem." In *The Collected Works of Langston Hughes*, edited by Arnold Rampersad, Vol. 1, 203–4. New York: Vintage Books, 2004.

wa Thiong'o, Ngugi. *The River Between*. New York: Heinemann, 1965.

Printed in the USA
CPSIA information can be obtained
at www.ICGtesting.com
LVHW011730260923
758848LV00006B/13